CW00541071

GREAT GIFTS

TO MAKE AND WRAP

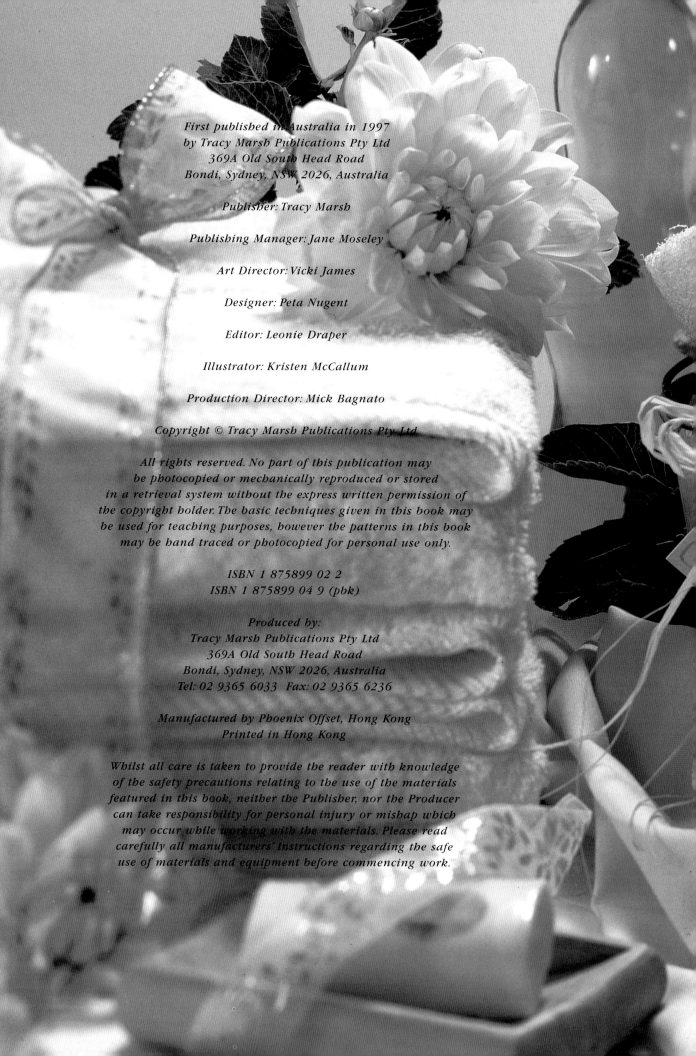

First published in Australia in 1997
by Tracy Marsh Publications Pty Ltd
369A Old South Head Road
Bondi, Sydney, NSW 2026, Australia

Publisher: Tracy Marsh

Publishing Manager: Jane Moseley

Art Director: Vicki James

Designer: Peta Nugent

Editor: Leonie Draper

Illustrator: Kristen McCallum

Production Director: Mick Bagnato

Copyright © Tracy Marsh Publications Pty Ltd

All rights reserved. No part of this publication may
be photocopied or mechanically reproduced or stored
in a retrieval system without the express written permission of
the copyright holder. The basic techniques given in this book may
be used for teaching purposes, however the patterns in this book
may be hand traced or photocopied for personal use only.

ISBN 1 875899 02 2
ISBN 1 875899 04 9 (pbk)

Produced by:
Tracy Marsh Publications Pty Ltd
369A Old South Head Road
Bondi, Sydney, NSW 2026, Australia
Tel: 02 9365 6033 Fax: 02 9365 6236

Manufactured by Phoenix Offset, Hong Kong
Printed in Hong Kong

Whilst all care is taken to provide the reader with knowledge
of the safety precautions relating to the use of the materials
featured in this book, neither the Publisher, nor the Producer
can take responsibility for personal injury or mishap which
may occur while working with the materials. Please read
carefully all manufacturers' instructions regarding the safe
use of materials and equipment before commencing work.

GREAT GIFTS
TO MAKE AND WRAP

CONTENTS

CONTENTS

$\mathcal{I}$NTRODUCTION

Nothing compares with the pleasure to be found in giving a handmade gift, unless, of course it's the exquisite delight felt when receiving such a gift. In this beautiful full color book you will find countless ideas for gifts which you can make, wrap and give, as well as suggestions for the particular occasions each gift may ideally suit.

Every project comes with easy-to-follow instructions, patterns where required, and a full color photograph of each finished piece. These easy-to-make projects use a mixture of recycled and new craft components and include all of the most popular craft techniques.

Once you have selected and made the gift to suit your needs, you can then turn to the gift wrapping ideas section of the book where a treasure trove of elegant, inexpensive suggestions will provide you with ideas for wrapping and presenting your creative gifts. This section of the book will inspire you with innovative ways to wrap, tie and decorate your handmade gifts ready for giving.

The book includes a free sheet of gift wrap and for each project there is a specially designed tag to complement the gift. The matching tag is shown on each project page—simply cut the required tag from the tear out pages at the back of the book and write on it your message.

To help you keep a record of the gifts you have made and given, we have provided a gift giving register. On page 87 of the book you can list the gifts which you have made and given for special occasions. There is also a space for noting particular dates which you don't want to forget.

Great Gifts to Make and Wrap will give you ideas for gifts to suit everyone, from the tiniest newborn to the person who seems to have just about everything. We feel sure you will derive endless enjoyment from making, wrapping and giving the beautiful and unusual gifts illustrated throughout this book.

ABOUT THIS BOOK

This book is set out to make it as easy as possible for you to immediately get started making and presenting gifts to those you love. This page explains the sections of the book and how to put them to good use. Happy gift giving!

GIFTS TO MAKE

WRAPPING AND PRESENTING GIFTS

The wrapping ideas section of the book offers you some suggestions on ways to make your own inexpensive but beautifully matched gift wraps. These ideas can be put to use for all your gifts.

Each project includes a list of the materials required, step-by-step instructions, and a full color photograph of the finished piece so that you can easily choose the right gift to make.

GIFT GIVING REGISTER, TAGS & WRAP

A free sheet of gift wrap and gift tags to suit every project are provided with the book. Use the gift giving register to keep a note of important dates and also to record which gifts you have made and given for various special occasions.

7

GIFTS TO MAKE

FRAGRANT LEMON CRAFTS

Lemons are an extremely versatile fruit with a refreshing fragrance. Any one of these gifts would be an ideal pick-me-up for someone convalescing after an illness.

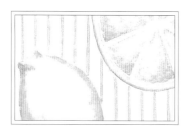

MATERIALS NEEDED

LEMON SOAPBALLS
- *soap powder*
- *lemon oil*
- *yellow vegetable dye*

LEMON POTPOURRI
- *lemon*
- *mixing bowl*
- *metal spoon or fork*
- *orris root powder*
- *lemon oil*
- *dried roses
  (buds & petals)*
- *yellow flowers:
  everlasting or globe
  amaranth*
- *dried leaves: rose
  or eucalyptus*
- *pine (casuarina) cones*
- *cinnamon sticks*
- *plastic bag*
- *bowl for display*

LEMON ROSEWATER
- *dried roses
  (buds & petals)*
- *mixing bowl*
- *strainer*
- *rose oil*
- *lemon*
- *glass jar*

LEMON SOAPBALLS

Mix the soap powder and the lemon oil together. Use approximately two thirds of a cup of soap powder to one teaspoon of fragrance.

Add one and a half teaspoons of water to the mix (enough so that the powder will compress easily). Add a little more water or more soap powder to achieve this consistency. A small amount of yellow vegetable dye can be added to color the mixture.

Divide the mixture into small portions then roll each piece into a smooth ball. Allow to dry. Drying time will depend on the size of the soapballs. As an alternative, the soap can also be pressed into moulds.

LEMON POTPOURRI

Potpourri can be made from just about anything you choose—this lemon potpourri has a light summery fragrance, perfect for freshening up a bedroom, bathroom or kitchen.

Lemons can be dried either in the oven or in the microwave. If using an oven, place the cut slices of one lemon on a baking tray and place in an oven set on low heat. Leave for approximately twenty minutes. If using a microwave, place the lemon slices on a sheet of absorbent towel. Microwave for five minutes until the lemons are dried. Be careful not to overdo it as they can easily burn.

A sunny day provides a natural alternative for drying your lemons. Place the cut slices of lemon or lemon peel on a tray behind a closed window. If left for a day or so, the heat from the glass will be sufficient to dry the lemon. This method also preserves the oils in the lemon skin.

To make the potpourri, place approximately two teaspoons of orris root powder in a large bowl. The orris root powder acts as a fixative for the fragrant oils used in potpourri. Add half a teaspoon of lemon oil to the powder and allow it to absorb. If the mixture appears too wet, add more orris root powder. Stir well. It is advisable to use an old metal kitchen spoon or fork rather than a wooden spoon as the wood will absorb and retain the fragrance.

Add a cup of dried roses, a cup of yellow flowers, some dried leaves and half a cup of pine cones to the bowl. Add five or six cinnamon sticks and the dried lemons. Stir all the ingredients well. Place the potpourri into a plastic bag and shake well.

The potpourri is ready for immediate use, place it in the bowl of your choice ready for giving. The mixture should be turned in the bowl occasionally to refresh the scent.

LEMON ROSEWATER

Put half a cup of dried roses into a mixing bowl. Pour two cups of boiling water over the roses and stir well. Allow the roses to infuse for a few hours. Filter the rosewater through a strainer and add a few drops of rose oil.

Strain the juice of one lemon and mix with the rosewater as follows: fill the glass jar with approximately two thirds rosewater and one third lemon juice and place in a refrigerator or keep in a cool place.

The lemon rosewater is a great skin tonic—for freshening up in warm weather—or you can scent clothing by putting a little in the washing water.

GILDED FLORAL ORNAMENTS

Real gold is traditionally associated with wishing people well at special times of life. Now, with the help of some inexpensive gilding materials you can give golden gifts at a comfortable price. Give these ornaments for a house warming or a new neighbor welcome.

GILDED POT

Wrap the latex molding around the rim of the terracotta pot, to measure the length required, then cut the piece to fit. Apply quick-drying glue to the surface of the molding then apply the molding around the rim of the pot (refer to the photograph on page 15). Remove it and wait for about five to ten minutes until the glue becomes sticky. Put the molding back on and apply a little pressure to it so that it adheres firmly to the rim of the pot. Leave to dry fully before proceeding to gild the pot.

Using the basecoat brush, apply the primer (brown or red earth acrylic paint) to the pot, in a thin, even coat. Traditionally this layer is known as a bole and it provides a strong colored background on which to lay the gold leaf, this enhances the richness of the final gilded coloring. Allow the painted surface to dry completely, this may take about thirty minutes.

Using a clean brush, apply the gilding size evenly all over the surface of the pot. The size is an adhesive for the gold leaf and is ready to accept the leaf when it becomes clear, this usually takes about twenty minutes.

To test whether the size is ready to accept the leaf, you lightly tap

MATERIALS NEEDED

GILDING
- *brushes: basecoat, soft-bristled*
- *acrylic primer: brown earth or red earth*
- *size*
- *cotton gloves*
- *gold Dutch metal leaf*
- *antiquing medium (or brown earth paint)*
- *sealer*
- *craft glue*

GILDED POT
- *terracotta pot*
- *latex molding trim to fit your pot*
- *quick-drying glue*
- *large oasis foam ball*
- *dried rose buds*

CHERUB VASE
- *bisque cherub with bowl*
- *large oasis foam ball*
- *dried rose buds*

your knuckle on the surface. Be careful not to touch the size with your finger as fingerprints remain in the size and will be visible beneath the fragile gold leaf.

Cut the sheets of gold leaf in half so that they are easier to handle. Wearing cotton gloves, carefully apply sheets of the leaf to the surface of the pot. The leaf will adhere to the size and cannot be removed and repositioned at this stage. Don't worry if the leaf tangles or creases as this only adds to the authentic look of the piece. Continue gilding until both the pot and the molding are fully covered with the gold leaf.

Using a clean brush, push the leaf into the crevices of the molding to ensure the leaf adheres to all the surfaces. Use skewings (left-over pieces of leaf) to fill in any gaps or, if preferred, you can allow small areas of the brown or red basecoat color to show through.

Using a clean dry brush, apply a coat of sealer (shellac can also be used) over the gilded leaf. This will protect the leaf from tarnishing and prepares the surface for antiquing.

When antiquing, it is not always necessary to use brown; colors such as black, white or verdigris can also produce interesting effects. Apply the paint with a soft paintbrush then wipe the excess off with a cloth. Allow the paint to gather in all the crevices of the molding as this will add to the antiqued effect. Leave the painted pot to dry thoroughly before proceeding.

To make the rose ball, firstly place craft clue around the inside of the pot and insert the oasis foam ball into the pot. Using the rose buds and starting at the base, push the stem of each rose bud into the foam, working your way around the pot. For the next line, insert the rose buds so that each one sits immediately above the small

ROSE BUD BALLS
Rose buds have a pretty, delicate look and their natural fragrance can be enhanced by a few drops of rose-scented oil.

14

GLUING ON THE MOLDING
The latex molding is cut to fit and then carefully glued around the rim of the pot.

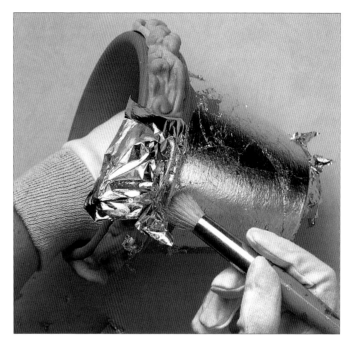

GILDING THE POT
Always work with gloves to ensure that you do not mark the gilded surface and diminish its glow.

space between two buds of the first row. In this way you will have an even spread of rose buds over the entire ball. Continue until the foam ball is completely covered.

CHERUB VASE

The bisque cherub is gilded following the technique described above. Place the oasis foam ball on top of the stand and glue to hold. You may need to cut a small slice off the bottom of the oasis foam ball so that it will sit flat on the stand. Cover the ball with dried rose buds as explained above.

APPLYING THE ROSE BUDS
The rose buds are applied to the oasis foam in straight lines around the ball, with each line of rose buds being set slightly off to one side so that they sit above the small space between two rose buds of the previous row.

$\mathscr{T}$APESTRY $\mathscr{C}$OATHANGERS

These coathangers combine the beauty of roses and the elegant craft of tapestry. They are feminine and functional and would make a perfect gift for a bridal shower, or a going away present for a young lady leaving home for the start of her new, adult life.

BEIGE COATHANGER

Refer to the graph for the beige coathanger in the pattern section and locate the centre point. Mark the centre of the canvas with a pin and begin stitching from that point using the threads as indicated by the symbols in the graph.

Each square in the graph represents one half cross stitch and each symbol represents which color thread is to be used.

Cut the thread to 20" (50cm) lengths and begin by holding the tail under a few stitches to secure. Avoid using knots as they will prevent the finished work from sitting flat. Continue working the design out towards the edges. Work all the stitches in the same direction, do not turn the canvas as you work.

When the design is complete, cut the backing fabric to match the shape, allowing ½" (1cm) extra around the edges. Trim off the extra fabric and canvas.

Place the fabric and backing fabric with right sides facing each other. Sew along the left and right sides allowing a small opening at the top to place the hanger through.

When sewn, turn the fabric right side out. Place it over the coathanger, pulling the top of the hanger through the hole. Fill with wadding until it is quite firm, then sew the opening together using slip stitch.

Sew the pink braid around the edges, starting from the top edge of the coathanger and working all the way around it.

Twirl the ribbon around the top part of the coathanger and work down until the entire wire hanger is fully covered.

To finish your coathanger, trim off any excess ribbon and attach a ribbon bow at the base of the coathanger's hook.

BLACK COATHANGER

Refer to the graph for the black coathanger in the pattern section and locate the centre point.

Cross stitch the design in the same way as specified above for the beige coathanger. When the stitched design is complete, make up the black coathanger following the instructions which are given above for making up the beige coathanger.

MATERIALS NEEDED

BEIGE COATHANGER
- *8" x 20" (20cm x 50cm) #14 Mono Canvas*
- *8" x 20" (20cm x 50cm) backing fabric*
- *Coats Anchor Tapisserie Wool: 9208, 9204, 9174, 9162, 8428, 8402, 8420, 8366, 8364, 9402 (see key on graph for quantities)*
- *3' x ½" wide (1m x 1cm wide) pink braid*
- *polyester filling*
- *pink ribbon*

BLACK COATHANGER
- *8" x 20" (20cm x 50cm) #14 Mono Canvas*
- *8" x 20" (20cm x 50cm) backing fabric*
- *Coats Anchor Tapisserie Wool: 9208, 9204, 9174, 9162, 8402, 8420, 8366, 8364, 8308, 8040, 8042, 9800 (see key on graph for quantities)*
- *3' x ½" wide (1m x 1cm wide) pink braid*
- *polyester filling*
- *pink ribbon*

HALF CROSS STITCH
This stitch is made by forming small diagonal stitches which are each sewn over a single fabric thread intersection. The reverse side of the fabric will show only a series of vertical lines.

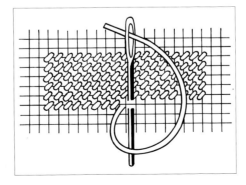

COVERED BOOKS

Fabric covered books are just right for storing favorite household hints, recipes, photographs or other memorabilia. You can make them as a gift for a birthday or as something special for Mothers' or Fathers' Day. Don't forget to write your inscription inside the book.

MATERIALS NEEDED
- *2 books: small, large*
- *foam or thin batting*
- *felt tipped pen*
- *scissors*
- *spray adhesive*
- *craft glue*
- *fabric*
- *gold braid*

Place a piece of foam on the work table and open the book out on top of it. Using a felt tipped pen, draw around the book onto the foam allowing extra for the spine. Using a sharp pair of scissors, cut out the piece of foam.

Place the book, opened out and face down, onto the table and apply the spray adhesive over the front and back of the book, including the spine. Place the foam on the front of the book, then across to the back, smoothing it down with your hand so it attaches properly. Allow to dry for a few minutes then trim back any overlapping edges. Using the fabric of your choice, place it pattern side down on the table and open the book, face up, on top. Again, use the pen to draw around the shape of the book, allowing a border of approximately 2" (5cm).

Cut out the piece of fabric. Ensuring there is a sufficient border of fabric around all edges, spray glue the fabric onto the back cover of the book. Glue the fabric onto the spine and front cover in the same way. Open the book to the inside front cover. Bring the two corners and the side fabric over onto the inside cover and stick down with craft glue. Make two small cuts in the fabric above and below the spine. Glue the top and bottom fabric onto the inside front and back covers.

Trim back the remaining fabric flaps at the top and bottom of the spine. Glue the first page of the book to the inside front cover and the last page to the inside back cover using craft glue. Embellish the books by gluing a gold braid trim around the edges to complete. On a plain fabric, you can also add small flowers, shells or charms to decorate the cover.

COVERING THE BOOK Make sure you leave an adequate amount of fabric around all edges of the book so that the covered book will have a neat and even finish.

STENCILED BATHROOM SET

Why not celebrate the successful renovation of a bathroom with this charming stenciled set of accessories? Choose colors to match the new bathroom scheme.

MATERIALS NEEDED

STENCILING
- *craft knife & mat*
- *stencil sheet & magic tape*
- *small stencil brush*
- *palette*
- *paper towel*

SOAP
- *fine steel wool*
- *white soap*
- *spray sealer*
- *acrylic paints: napthol crimson, raw sienna, green oxide*

HAND TOWEL
- *white hand towel*
- *textile medium (or fabric paints)*
- *acrylic paints: napthol crimson, raw sienna, green oxide*
- *spray sealer*
- *gingham ribbon: red and white*

BUCKET
- *6" (16cm) metal bucket*
- *800 wet-and-dry sandpaper*
- *water-based rustproof etched primer*
- *basecoating brush*
- *cream acrylic basecoat*
- *acrylic paints: napthol crimson, raw sienna, green oxide, pearl white, rich gold*
- *sponge*
- *spray sealer*

PREPARATION

Transfer the design from the pattern section onto the stencil sheet. Carefully cut out the stencil using a craft knife and mat.

SOAP

Using the fine steel wool, lightly sand the top surface of the soap to smooth the surface. Apply one coat of spray sealer and allow to dry.

Select an individual apple to stencil or, if the soap is large, group two apples together. Position the stencil over the soap and use magic tape to hold in position.

Dip the stencil brush into the napthol crimson and swirl the brush on the palette to work the paint well into the bristles. Wipe the excess paint off onto a paper towel so that the brush is dry.

Apply the paint through the cut stencil, working in a circular motion around the stencil, gradually building up the depth of color. Use raw sienna to paint the stalk and green oxide to paint the leaf. Allow to dry then apply a coat of spray sealer.

HAND TOWEL

Pre-wash the hand towel to remove any fixatives or chemicals. Mix the textile medium with the paints at a 1:1 ratio. Textile medium added to the paints prevents the colors from fading or running when the towel is washed, it also reduces bleeding of the paints under the stencil.

Put the apple stencil about 4" (10cm) above the bottom of the towel and use magic tape to hold in place. Following the instructions given for the soap, apply the paint through the stencil. Allow to dry. Heat-set the paint by ironing the towel on the reverse side.

Sew a length of thin red and white gingham trim to the towel.

BUCKET

The bucket used in this project is new metal so there is no problem with rust. If you are using an old bucket, you must ensure that any rust is completely removed. Using dry 800 wet-and-dry sandpaper, sand the surface of the bucket lightly. Apply two coats of water-based rustproof etched primer. The primer must be water-based to work well with the water-based paints that are used for basecoating and stenciling.

Using the basecoating brush, apply three coats of cream basecoat to adequately cover the rust colored primer. Allow to dry.

To quick cure the paint, pre-heat the oven to 250°F (120°C). Place the painted bucket in the oven and leave for 15-20 minutes. Turn off the oven and allow it to cool before removing the bucket from the oven.

Position the stencil around the centre of the bucket and secure using magic tape. Following the instructions given for the soap, apply the paint through the stencil. Remove the stencil and reposition it on the other side of the bucket, stenciling as before. Allow to dry.

Dip the dry sponge into pearl white and sponge around the apple design. Use rich gold to paint the handle and the rim around the bottom of the bucket. When dry, apply one coat of spray sealer.

ETCHED BOWL

For an engagement or wedding gift that will be treasured and used forever, you cannot go past this exquisite etched bowl. As an extra personal touch, you could etch the initials of the happy couple in as part of the design. Choose an image which fits the occasion for which the gift is being given.

The straight sides of this glass bowl make this the perfect piece for beginners to glass etching. Bowls like this one can be found at any large department or variety store. You can use any pre-cut stencil that suits your bowl and the occasion to be celebrated, or cut your own stencil from one of the patterns given in the pattern section of this book.

Wash the bowl with soap and water then dry thoroughly. Using the spray adhesive, lightly spray the back of the stencil and allow a few seconds for it to become tacky. Carefully position the stencil in place on the side of the bowl. Smooth the stencil down onto the glass to ensure that it has adhered to the glass. This is important because if the cream is allowed to bleed under the stencil, it will etch areas that it is not supposed to. Use adhesive tape on each end of the stencil to prevent the ends from lifting away from the surface of the glass during stenciling.

When handling the etching cream wear rubber gloves. Use an old kitchen or palette knife to apply the cream and to smooth it out, being careful not to overlap the edges of the stencil. Leave the cream to work for 15-20 minutes or as specified by the manufacturer.

Use the knife to remove the excess cream from the stencil and return this to the bottle. This can be reused so very little is wasted. Wipe the remaining cream from the surface with a damp kitchen sponge and rinse the sponge clean.

Hold the bowl, with the stencil still in place, under warm running water to remove any cream that may still be on the surface then remove the stencil. Wipe the surface with a clean sponge and dry.

Repeat the stencil around the bowl as many times as desired, each time ensuring the stencil is firmly adhered to the glass surface.

The same technique can be used to decorate drinking glasses, glass platters, vases and mirrors.

MATERIALS NEEDED

- *glass bowl*
- *spray adhesive*
- *pre-cut stencil*
- *adhesive tape*
- *rubber gloves*
- *etching cream*
- *palette knife*
- *kitchen sponge*

*ETCHING CREAM
Be sure to wear gloves and follow the manufacturer's instructions when working with etching cream.*

𝒦NITTED ℬEARS

On any occasion, the young and the young at heart will be delighted to receive these adorable bears. They would make a memorable gift for a newborn or a special treasure for an older child celebrating the arrival of a new sibling.

MATERIALS NEEDED

- *Patons Dream Time Baby Wool 3 ply Shade 51 (cream): 4 x 1 oz (25g) balls*
- *1st Contrast (C1): Shade 3132 (blue) x 1 ball (Standing Bear)*
- *2nd Contrast (C2): Shade 3129 (pink) x 1 ball (Sitting Bear)*
- *1 pair each no.10 (3.25mm) & no.12 (2.75mm) knitting needles (or whatever sizes are needed to give correct tension)*
- *polyester filling*
- *stranded cotton for features: grey (400) x 1 skein*
- *5' (1.5m) of ribbon*

Wool quantities given above are approximate as they vary between knitters.

It is important to use only the yarns specified for these items. Other yarns may give unsatisfactory results.

Although both these gorgeous bears are shown sitting down in our photograph, the instructions given here will enable you to make two different kinds of bears. The legs of each bear are attached differently so that the Sitting Bear can only sit down, whereas the Standing Bear is made in a upright position but can be made to sit down too, as shown in the photograph opposite. We have made these bears as a color co-ordinated pair. You can make either one or both of these endearing bears in the colors of your choice.

ABBREVIATIONS

alt = alternate; beg = beginning; in = inches; cm = centimetres; cont = continue; dec = decrease, decreasing; foll = follows, following; garter st = every row knit; inc = increase; "Inc" = knit into each of the 2 strands of next st (thus making 2 sts out of 1); incl = inclusive, including; K = knit; 0 = (zero) - no sts, rows or times; P = purl; patt = pattern; psso = pass slipped st over; purl fabric (reverse stocking st) = 1 row purl (right side), 1 row knit (wrong side); st/s = stitch/es; stocking st = 1 row knit, 1 row purl; sl = slip; "sl2 tog" = slip next 2 sts as if to K2tog; tbl = through back of loop; tog = together; ybk = yarn back - take yarn under needle from purling position into knitting position; yfwd = yarn forward - bring yarn under needle, then over into knitting position again, thus making a stitch; yon = yarn over needle - take yarn over top of

needle into knitting position, thus making a stitch; yrn = yarn round needle - take yarn right round needle into purling position, thus making a stitch.

MEASUREMENTS

The Standing Bear is roughly 12" (31cm) high. The Sitting Bear is about 9" (22cm) high (from the base of the body to the top of the head).

TENSION

27 sts and 38 rows to 4" (10cm) over stocking st, using no.10 (3.25mm) needles and yarn double.

Please check your tension carefully. If less sts use smaller needles, if more sts use bigger needles. To achieve the desired effect, these toys have been designed to be worked on smaller needles and at a tighter tension than usually recommended.
Note - the yarn is used double throughout.

TO MAKE HEAD *(beg at back)*
Using no.10 (3.25mm) needles and M double, cast on 8 sts.
1st row: ("Inc") 8 times ... 16 sts.
2nd and alt rows: Purl.
3rd row: K1, ("M1", K2) 7 times, "M1", K1.
5th row: K1, ("M1", K3) 7 times, "M1", K2.
7th row: K2, ("M1", K4) 7 times, "M1", K2.
Cont inc in this manner in alt rows until there are 80 sts. Tie a colored thread at each end of the last row to mark the position of the body. Work 13 rows stocking st, (beg with a purl row).

Shape Head

1st row: K6, (K2tog) 13 times, K16, (sl 1, K1, psso) 13 times, K6 ... 54 sts.

2nd and alt rows: Purl.

3rd row: (K16, "sl2 tog", K1, psso) twice, K16.

5th row: K15, "sl2 tog", K1, psso, K14, "sl2 tog", K1, psso, K15.

7th row: K14, "sl2 tog", K1, psso, K12, "sl2 tog", K1, psso, K14.

Cont dec in this manner in alt rows until 30 sts rem. Tie a colored thread around 12th st from each end of last row to mark position of eyes.

Next row: P1, ("M1", P2) 5 times, "M1", P8, "M1", (P2, "M1") 5 times, P1 ... 42 sts.

Shape Nose

1st row: K1, * K2tog, K13, sl 1, K1, psso *, K6, rep from * to * once, K1.

2nd and alt rows: Purl.

3rd row: K1, * K2tog, K11, sl 1, K1, psso *, K6, rep from * to * once, K1.

5th row: K1, * K2tog, K9, sl 1, K1, psso *, K6, rep from * to * once, K1.

7th row: K1, * K2tog, K7, sl 1, K1, psso *, K6, rep from * to * once, K1.

9th row: K1, * K2tog, K5, sl 1, K1, psso *, K6, rep from * to * once, K1 ... 22sts.

11th row: K1, (sl 1, K1, psso) 5 times, (K2tog) 5 times, K1 ... 12 sts.

13th row: (sl 1, K1, psso) 3 times, (K2tog) 3 times ... 6 sts. Break off yarn, run end through rem sts, draw up tightly and fasten off securely.

NOSE (beg at top)

Using no.10 (3.25mm) needles and C1 double for Standing Bear or C2 double for Sitting Bear, cast on 7 sts. Work 2 rows stocking st.

3rd row: K1, K2tog, K1, sl 1, K1, psso, K1 ... 5 sts.

Work 2 rows stocking st.

Break off yarn, run end through rem sts, draw up tightly and fasten off securely.

OUTER EARS (beg at bottom)

Using no.10 (3.25mm) needles and M double, cast on 18 sts.

1st row: K1, "Inc", K5, ("Inc") 4 times, K5, "Inc", K1 ... 24 sts.

Work 3 rows stocking st (beg with a purl row).

5th row: K1, K2tog, knit to last 3 sts, sl 1, K1, psso, K1.

6th row: Purl.

Rep 5th and 6th rows 3 times ... 16 sts. Cast off.

INNER EARS

Using no.12 (2.75mm) needles and C1 double for Standing Bear or C2 double for Sitting Bear, work as for Outer Ears.

BODY (beg at top)

Using no.10 (3.25mm) needles and M double, cast on 30 sts.

1st row: K5, ("Inc") 20 times, K5 ... 50 sts.

Work 11 rows stocking st (beg with a purl row).

13th row: K11, ("Inc") 4 times, K20, ("Inc") 4 times, K11 ... 58 sts.

Work 19 rows stocking st.

33rd row: K12, (sl 1, K1, psso) 4 times, K18, (K2tog) 4 times, K12 ... 50 sts.

Work 5 rows stocking st.

39th row: K10, (sl 1, K1, psso) 4 times, K14, (K2tog) 4 times, K10 ... 42 sts.

If making Sitting Bear, tie a colored thread around the 10th st from each end of last row to mark position of the legs.

Work 4 rows stocking st.

Shape Lower Body

(NOTE - When turning, bring yarn to front of work, slip next st on to right-hand needle, ybk, slip st back on to left-hand needle, then turn and proceed as instructed - this avoids holes in the work.)

1st row: P12, turn.

2nd row: K12.

3rd row: P11, P2tog, purl to end.

4th row: K12, turn.

5th row: P12.

6th row: K11, sl 1, K1, psso, knit to end.

Rep 1st and 2nd rows once.

9th row: P11, (P2tog) twice, purl to end.

Rep 4th and 5th rows once.

12th row: K11, (sl 1, K1, psso) twice, knit to end ... 36 sts.

13th row: (P2tog) 18 times.

14th row: (K2tog) 9 times.

Break off yarn, run end through rem sts, draw up tightly and fasten off securely.

RIGHT LEG (beg at sole)

Using no.10 (3.25mm) needles and M double, cast on 26 sts.

1st row: K8, ("Inc") 4 times, K8, ("Inc") 4 times, K2.

2nd and 4th rows: Purl.

3rd row: K10, ("Inc") 4 times, K12, ("Inc") 4 times, K4.

5th row: K12, ("Inc") 4 times, K16, ("Inc") 4 times, K6 ... 50 sts.

Work 11 rows stocking st (beg with a purl row).

17th row: K6, (sl 1, K1, psso) 5 times, (K2tog) 5 times, K10, (sl 1, K1, psso) twice, (K2tog) twice, K6.

18th row: Purl.

19th row: K5, (sl 1, K1, psso) 3 times, (K2 tog) 3 times, K19 ... 30 sts.

Work 11 rows stocking st.

31st row: - K9, ("Inc") twice, K11, ("Inc") twice, K6 ... 34 sts.

** Work 7 rows stocking st.

Shape Top

Cast off 4 sts at beg of next 2 rows.

Dec at each end of next and alt rows until 18 sts rem, then in every row until 12 sts rem.

Next row: (K2tog) 6 times.

Break off yarn, run end through rem sts, draw up tightly and fasten off securely.

LEFT LEG (beg at sole)

Using no.10 (3.25mm) needles and M double, cast on 26 sts.

1st row: K2, ("Inc") 4 times, K8, ("Inc") 4 times, K8.

2nd and 4th rows: Purl.

3rd row: K4, ("Inc") 4 times, K12, ("Inc") 4 times, K10.

5th row: K6, ("Inc") 4 times, K16, ("Inc") 4 times, K12 ... 50 sts.

Work 11 rows stocking st (beg with a purl row).

17th row: K6, (sl 1, K1, psso) twice, (K2 tog) twice, K10, (sl 1, K1, psso) 5 times, (K2tog) 5 times, K6.

18th row: Purl

19th row: K19, (sl 1, K1, psso) 3 times, (K2tog) 3 times, K5 ... 30 sts.
Work 11 rows stocking st.
31st row: K6, ("Inc") twice, K11, ("Inc") twice, K9 ... 34 sts.
Complete as for Right Leg from ** to end.

FOOT PADS (make 2)
Using no. 10 (3.25mm) needles and C1 double for Standing Bear or C2 double for Sitting Bear, cast on 5 sts.
1st row: K1, ("Inc", K1) twice.
2nd row: Purl.
3rd row: K1, "Inc", K3, "Inc", K1 ... 9 sts.
Work 15 rows stocking st (beg with a purl row).
19th row: K1, K2tog, K3, sl 1, K1, psso, K1.
20th row: Purl.
21st row: K1, K2tog, K1, sl 1, K1, psso, K1 ... 5 sts.
Cast off purlways.

ARMS (make 2 beg at hand)
Using no. 10 (3.25mm) needles and M double, cast on 15 sts.
1st row: K1, * "Inc", K1, rep from * to end ... 22 sts.
Work 13 rows stocking st (beg with a purl row).
15th row: K9, ("Inc") 4 times, K9 ... 26 sts.
Work 21 rows stocking st.
Shape Top
Dec at each end of next 5 rows, then foll alt row ... 14 sts.
Work 1 row.
Next row: (K2tog) 7 times.
Break off yarn, run end through rem sts, draw up tightly and fasten off securely.

HAND PADS (make 2)
Work as for Foot Pads, working 7 rows stocking st instead of 15.

MAKE UP
Run a thread through the cast-on sts of head, draw up tightly and fasten off securely. Using running st, join the seam, leaving an opening in the centre for filling (this seam will be underneath the head). Transfer the colored threads on the seam line to the outside. Fill firmly, pushing the filling well into the nose, then join the opening. Using back stitch, join the outer and inner ear pieces tog, leaving cast-on edge open. Turn to right side and oversew cast-on edges tog, then sew ears in position as illustrated, curving slightly and leaving approximately 2½" (6.5cm) between them.

Using bullion stitch and stranded cotton, embroider the eyes at the points marked by colored threads. Sew the nose in position, inserting a small amount of filling into the nose. Using straight stitch and stranded cotton, embroider the mouth as illustrated. Using running stitch, join the body seam, leaving the cast-on edge open. Fill firmly.

Place the head on the cast-on edge of the body, pinning the colored threads on the head seam to the centre back seam of the body. Pin rem of cast-on edge of body to the head and sew in position, pushing more filling into the body if necessary before completing the seam. Using running stitch, join the leg seams, then fold the leg so that the seam is at the inside leg position and join the cast-on edge with a flat seam. Fill firmly.

For Standing Bear: pin the tops of the legs to the centre of first set of dec sts on body, and top of the leg seam to base of body beside the gathered up sts, then pin rem of open leg edge to body. Sew in position as pinned, pushing in more filling if necessary.

For Sitting Bear: place base of body on flat surface. Pin the top of the legs to the colored threads on the body, then pin rem of open leg edge to body with legs placed at right angles to body. Check that the Bear will sit up properly, adjusting position of legs if necessary. There should be approximately 8 sts between the legs at the front of the body. Sew in position as pinned, pushing more filling in as necessary.

For Both Bears: run a thread through cast-on sts of arms, draw up tightly and fasten off securely. Using running stitch, join arm seams, leaving top shaped edges open. Fill firmly. Pin the arms to the body, placing the top edge approximately two rows below the neck and top of arm seam to centre of inc sts on body. Sew in position as pinned, pushing more filling as needed. Oversew the foot and hand pads in position. Tie a pretty bow around each bear's neck.

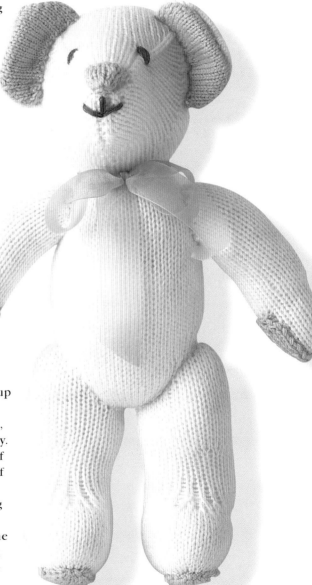

Sculpted Terracotta Daisy Pots

A gift for use in the garden is most welcome at any time of the year. These pots would be ideal for a house warming, harvest festival, birthday, or even as a Christmas gift.

MATERIALS NEEDED

- *terracotta pots*
- *blue acrylic paint*
- *sealer*
- *sponge brush*
- *molding clay: white, yellow*
- *scissors*
- *rolling pin*
- *tracing paper*
- *pencil*
- *craft knife & mat*
- *aluminium foil*
- *baking tray*
- *craft glue*

Wash each terracotta pot with warm soapy water to remove any dirt or dust and allow to dry. Mix the blue paint with equal parts of the sealer and paint the desired area of the pot (refer to the photograph for ideas). Using the sponge brush, apply two or three coats of the paint mix. Allow to dry.

From the pattern section, trace daisy shapes (as many as needed) onto tracing paper and cut each one out. Lightly knead the white molding clay and, using the rolling pin, roll out to about 1/8" (3mm) thick. Place the cut out daisy petal shapes onto the rolled out molding clay. Using the craft knife, cut the molding clay around the paper shape, remove the paper and smooth the edges. Roll a small ball of yellow molding clay and press it flat. Arrange the petals into a daisy shape and place the flattened yellow piece in the centre, pressing gently to ensure the pieces adhere to one another.

To make small daisies, roll four small balls of white molding clay and press them flat so they join one another in a circle. Roll a small yellow ball and press it into the centre.

Make some daisies with reverse colorings, i.e. white centres on a yellow background.

Place the formed daisies on a baking tray lined with aluminium foil and bake in a preheated oven at 275°F (135°C) for 10 minutes. Allow them to cool.

Attach the daisies to the terracotta pots with the craft glue.

Before using the pots they must be coated inside with a strong sealer to prevent moisture in the soil from affecting the paint finish. Alternatively you can place a plastic pot inside each of the terracotta pots before planting in them.

SHAPING THE DAISIES
Roughly cut the petal shapes from the rolled out molding clay with a scalpel. Gently mold the edges to create the rounded petal tips.

HERB & GARLIC WREATH

This cheerful, healthy wreath is just what the doctor ordered when you want to help a loved one to get well soon. A slight, fresh scent is provided by the use of fragrant cinnamon sticks around the wreath.

Arrange a layer of Spanish moss around the entire wreath and glue it into place. Break off five small sprigs of eucalyptus leaves and position them around the wreath evenly, glue in place. Glue a few bay leaves alongside each of the sprigs of eucalyptus.

Cut the ribbon into five lengths of 18" (45cm). Take a length and hold it between the thumb and forefinger about 1½" (4cm) from the end. Loop the ribbon backwards and forwards from the top to the bottom to create loops each 3" (7.5cm) long (see photograph 1). Hold firmly and wrap a piece of florists' wire around the centre. Fold the ribbon up around the florists' wire and pinch firmly to hold (see photograph 2). Trim off excess wire with wire cutters. Glue one ribbon bow beside each of the five eucalyptus sprigs.

Arrange and glue the cloves of garlic onto the wreath between the bows. Pull some cloves off the bulb and glue them onto the wreath individually. The bottom section of the cloves or bulbs can be trimmed flat to enable easier gluing.

Arrange and glue cinnamon sticks around the wreath.

MATERIALS NEEDED

- 8" (20cm) wreath
- Spanish moss
- hot glue gun & glue sticks
- eucalyptus leaves
- bay leaves
- 6½' x 4" wide (2.25m x 10mm wide) red checked ribbon
- scissors
- florists' wire
- sticks of cinnamon
- wire cutters
- garlic cloves

1. FORMING THE LOOPS
Fold the ribbon length concertina-style so that it forms several even-sized loops and so that the trailing ends are both of similar lengths.

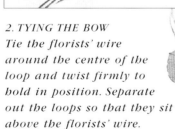

2. TYING THE BOW
Tie the florists' wire around the centre of the loop and twist firmly to hold in position. Separate out the loops so that they sit above the florists' wire.

$\mathscr{W}$ILBUR $\mathscr{P}$IG
Every child needs a special pal to play with and Wilbur Pig is a wonderfully warm and cuddly friend. For a birthday, Christmas, or sibling present on the arrival of a new babe: Wilbur's the one.

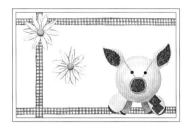

MATERIALS NEEDED

- *tracing paper & pencil*
- *28" x 24" (70cm x 60cm) fleecy cotton fabric*
- *8" (20cm) floral fabric (for trotters, snout and ears)*
- *polyester filling*
- *1 piece florists' wire*
- *black & cream cotton*
- *2 small black buttons (for eyes)*
- *fabric scraps & buttons*
- *8" x 8" (20cm x 20cm) fusible webbing*
- *small amount of raffia*
- *hot glue gun & glue sticks*

P re-wash the fleecy cotton fabric and the floral fabric before use: the completed pig can then be safely washed without shrinking. Trace the pattern for Wilbur Pig from the pattern section and cut out all the pattern pieces. Note that some of the pieces are cut from fleecy cotton fabric and some are cut from the floral fabric. (You can use a checked or spotted fabric instead of a floral fabric for the trotters, snout and ears.) Pin the pattern to the specified fabrics and cut out the fabric pieces.

Placing the right sides of the underbody together, stitch from A-B. Place A of the underbody in line with A of the body, stitch the underbody to the body, A-F, G-G, F-F. Sew the trotters to the pig, F-G. Stitch the body pieces together, H-C, leaving the end, H-A, open for stuffing. Stitch the head gusset between front and back body pieces, D-C-D.

Gather the snout end and slip stitch closed. Join the snout seam on the straight piece of fleecy cotton fabric. Sew to the fabric snout, easing the fabric to fit.

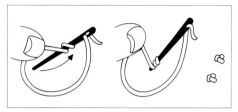

FRENCH KNOTS

Stuff the snout with polyester filling, lightly gather and close. Using black cotton, make two French knots for the nostrils. Sew into position by hand.

Fill the pig's body and slip stitch the opening closed, gather to fit, H-A.

Fold tail in half, right sides facing, sew a seam and turn to right side. Bend the florists' wire in half and place it in the tail so it curls up. Attach the tail to the pig.

Sew right side of each fabric ear to right side of a fleecy ear, leaving straight edges open. Turn to the right side and turn under 1/4" (6mm) on the lower edge and slip stitch closed. Sew in place on the head. Sew on the two small black buttons for the eyes.

Using small scraps of different colored and patterned fabrics, add the patchwork to the pig. Iron squares of fusible webbing to the fabric scraps, using an iron on a low setting. Place the fusible webbing, paper side up, on the wrong side of the material. Glide the iron across the paper side for 1-2 seconds. Allow the material to cool then cut the fabric into small squares. Peel off the backing paper and then position and iron onto the pig.

Thread buttons with a few strands of cream cotton, tie off and cut the ends. Attach buttons and small raffia bows around the tail and on the side of the head using the hot glue gun. (Omit buttons for smaller children.)

STAMP PAD STENCILING

For those particularly special occasions when you want to personalise a gift, stencil up something unique with colors and images to suit the celebration at hand.

MATERIALS NEEDED

- *pre-cut stencils*
- *spray adhesive*
- *masking tape*
- *scissors*
- *round synthetic sponges*
- *multicolor stamp pad*
- *embossing powder*
- *spray sealer*

Stamp pads offer a quick and easy way of applying colors to stencils of your choice. Here, the technique is explained and some wonderful suggestions are given on ways to use this technique to create beautiful personalised gifts.

HOW TO STAMP PAD STENCIL

Spray the back of the stencil with spray adhesive, allow to dry slightly so that it is sticky to touch then press onto the piece to be stenciled, smoothing it down so it sticks firmly to the surface. Alternatively, you may keep it in place with masking tape. If necessary, use masking tape to mask off the surrounding areas, isolating the area you are planning to stencil.

Cut a round sponge into four pieces. Take a piece of sponge and, holding the pointed end, dab the rounded end into the required color on the stamp pad. When working on a multicolored pad, be careful to pick up only the desired color on the sponge. Use a separate piece of sponge for each color.

Using a circular motion, apply the color to the chosen area of the stencil. Repeat this procedure until the desired depth of color is achieved.

Overlays of accent colors can be applied and blended to selected areas to achieve a more realistic shaded appearance. For example, apply orange over a yellow base for a pear then shade with brown, or apply blue over a purple base for grapes.

If working on timber, be careful not to smudge the ink before it has completely dried. When complete, protect the timber by sealing it with a matt or gloss spray sealer.

IDEAS FOR STAMP PAD STENCILING

Wooden items such as place mats and coasters are ideal for stenciling in colors and patterns to co-ordinate with the dining room décor of the lucky recipient of the gift.

Ornaments, like the wooden wheelbarrow pictured here, can be stenciled and given for display or for some practical and decorative purpose such as a fruit bowl or as a container for a beautiful dried flower arrangement.

Any books with a plain cover, or books you have covered in plain paper, can be stenciled and given to be used as recipe books, address books, or diaries.

Stenciling onto brown or plain paper offers unlimited possibilities. Brown paper bags (large and small) are great for wrapping up relishes, sauces or wine bottles. Tie them up with a pretty raffia bow.

Using adhesive labels or plain paper, you can also stencil decorative labels and lid covers for your bottled homemade produce.

Larger pieces of paper can be stenciled with a border or with an all-over pattern and then used for wrapping paper.

Stencil matching gift tags on small pieces of cardboard and attach to the present using ribbon or raffia.

If you are working on paper or card with pigment inks you can achieve a beautiful glossy finish simply by sprinkling embossing powder over the stenciled areas. Shake off any excess powder and place the stenciled item over a toaster or other heat source to melt the powder to a shiny finish.

PAINTED GLASSWARE
These charming pieces, which look just like real stained glass, can be made from any attractive glassware you have available. They are just the thing for a house warming gift, an anniversary, to welcome a new neighbor, or to donate as a prize for a raffle.

Clean the jars with a warm water and white vinegar solution 1:1. Rinse them then towel them dry with a lint-free cloth. Trace the designs for the small and large jars from the pattern section onto tracing paper. Enlarge or reduce each design to fit onto the jars you have selected.

Position the designs on the inside of each jar in the required position so that the design is visible through the glass and tape in place to hold. If the neck of any jar is too narrow and will not allow the insertion of the traced design (as for the large jar used here), use graphite paper between the jar and the pattern and trace the design using a stylus or biro. Handle the jar with care to avoid erasing the graphite lines.

Using the black relief paint, follow the design lines and squeeze the tube gently between the thumb and forefinger to pipe an even raised line over all the outlines. Keep the end of the tip clean, wiping frequently. Any unevenness in the piped line can be corrected by sweeping a pin through the wet paint.

The relief paint forms the 'leading' of the stained glass design and provides a barrier inside which to paint the colors.

Make sure all the lines are fully connected with no gaps or the glass paint will escape into another section. Leave the outline to dry for approximately one hour, or as specified by the manufacturer.

Work in alternate sections of the design so that if the paint spills over into the wrong area it will not mix with another color. Flood each petal of the poinsettia with the burgundy glass paint, taking the paint right up to and touching the black lines. Fill each section to the top of the line. Use a pin to help push the paint into the corners.

If the color does spill over, clean it up with a cotton bud. If any bubbles form, use a pin to pop them. Allow the painted sections to dry slightly then go back and paint in the unpainted areas. Paint the centre of the poinsettia with orange paint. Leave the jar to dry on a flat surface.

Squeeze a small amount of avocado glass paint onto the palette. Using the flat brush, dip it into the green paint and apply it to the horizontal areas on the edge of the design. Press the brush down onto the glass and then lift off. Reload the brush and press the next stroke below the first. Continue reloading and pressing the paint to the glass along the horizontal areas of the design. This creates a textured, frosted look with a brick-like pattern.

With a small amount of gold glass paint on the palette, paint the small corner sections of the design in the same manner. Ensure the paint is applied right up to and touching the black lines.

Leave the completed paintwork to dry for 24 hours. Allow seven days for the paintwork to cure.

Painted glassware should only be washed by hand in warm soapy water; do not soak the glassware or place the items in the dishwasher. Dry with a soft towel. Enclose a note outlining these care instructions when you present the gift.

MATERIALS NEEDED

- *2 jars: small, large*
- *tracing paper*
- *pencil*
- *lint-free cloth*
- *graphite paper*
- *stylus*
- *relief paint: black*
- *palette*
- *glass paints: burgundy, orange, gold, avocado*
- *pins*
- *cotton buds*
- *adhesive tape*
- *small flat brush*

BREAD DOUGH FORGET-ME-NOTS

Forget-me-nots are a symbol of eternal care and so they make the ideal gift for a new mother, or for an engagement, a coming of age, or a leaving home present.

MATERIALS NEEDED

BREAD DOUGH
- *1 slice white bread (crusts removed)*
- *woodworking glue*
- *acrylic paints: white, mauve, yellow*
- *rolling pin*
- *flower cutter: 6 petals as used for cake decorating*
- *bowl, fork & pin*
- *sealer & plastic wrap*

BROOCH
- *jump ring, tiny heart & brooch back*
- *woodworking glue*
- *green dough*
- *4 bread dough leaves*
- *4 bread dough flowers*
- *4 large pearl stamens*

CARD
- *gold pen & white card*
- *woodworking glue*
- *3 bread dough flowers*
- *1 small gold bow*

FRAME
- *woodworking glue*
- *picture frame*
- *polyester wadding*
- *4" (10cm) cream silk*
- *needle & thread*
- *3 bread dough flowers*
- *4 bread dough leaves*
- *5 large pearl stamens*
- *gold bow*
- *cardboard*

To make the bread dough, crumb the bread and place the crumbs into a bowl. Drizzle woodworking glue over the crumbs and mix with a fork to make a firm dough. Add more crumbs if necessary. Hand knead the mixture to ensure there are no lumps. Keep the dough wrapped in plastic unless it is to be used immediately.

Divide the dough into halves. Add a small amount of white paint and some mauve paint to one half of the dough. Knead the color into the dough to achieve an even blend. Add and mix in more paint for a deeper shade if desired.

Break a small piece of dough from the second half and add yellow paint to it. This is to make the flower centres so it need only be a tiny piece. Mix a small amount of green paint into the remaining dough and knead it well in until it is evenly mixed.

To shape each leaf, break off a small piece of green dough and roll it into a ball between your thumb and finger. Squash the base gently and pinch the tip to form a leaf shape. Using the tip of a pin, draw in the veins on the leaf. Make eight leaves to complete the projects presented here.

To shape the flowers, roll out the mauve dough with a rolling pin until it is almost paper thin. Using a cake decorating cutter with six petals, cut out ten flowers. Draw the lines on each petal with a pin.

Place a tiny dot (the size of a pin head) of yellow dough in the centre of each flower and push it into place using a pin. Shape some of the petals upwards to give the flowers depth.

Wrap the leftover dough in plastic, you will need to use some of it when making the items shown below.

Allow the dough flowers and leaves to dry in a warm place for about twelve hours.

BROOCH
Thread the jump ring through the tiny heart and attach it to the brooch. Close the jump ring. Glue a small ball of green dough into the base of the brooch. Place three leaves onto the base and glue into place. Glue three forget-me-nots in position. Cut the ends off the pearl stamens and glue three around the flowers. Glue a flower, a leaf and a stamen into position on the tiny heart. Allow to dry. Apply one coat of sealer, ensuring the flowers and the leaves are all completely covered.

CARD
Position three flowers on the card. Using a gold pen, draw a flower stem from each flower head down the centre of the card. Glue the flowers into position. Glue the bow mid-way down the flower stems. Seal the three bread dough flowers with one coat of sealer. Add a spray of gold dots and outline the card with the gold pen.

PICTURE FRAME
Cut the cardboard into an oval shape to fit the centre of the frame. Insert the cardboard in the frame and glue

into place to form a backing.

Cut another piece of cardboard the same shape, though slightly smaller. Cut the polyester wadding to match the size and shape of the smaller cardboard.

Glue the wadding and the cardboard together. Lay the silk face down and position the cardboard on top of it. Trim the fabric around the cardboard, leaving an allowance of about $1/4$" (6mm).

Using a needle and thread, stitch running stitch around the edge of the silk and draw up over the wadding and cardboard. Tie the thread off.

Glue the flowers, leaves and stamen ends onto the silk. Position the gold bow under the flowers and glue into place. Carefully apply one coat of sealer to all the bread dough items. Allow to dry.

Apply woodworking glue to the backing cardboard area of the frame and press the picture into place. Press firmly until the glue has dried.

RIBBON ROSE BASKET VICTORIAN FRAME

This beautiful piece can be made for any special occasion. It would be ideal to celebrate an anniversary or to give for a special birthday present to a loved one.

MATERIALS NEEDED

- *rectangular photo frame*
- *piece of silk fabric to fit your frame*
- *spray adhesive*
- *hot glue gun & glue sticks*
- *pencil*
- *gold spray paint*
- *wooden basket cutout*
- *4" (10cm) of gold mesh ribbon*
- *28" (70cm) of gold braid*
- *20" (50cm) of narrow gold ribbon*
- *2' (60cm) of gold cord*
- *wire-edged ribbon: 5' (1.5m) each of cream and pink, 5 ³/₄' (1.7m) of green*
- *florists' wire*
- *4" (10cm) of green pearl yardage*
- *brass locket charm*

Carefully prise the front off the photo frame. Spray a light, even coat of adhesive over the upper surface of the back section and press the silk fabric on smoothly.

Use the glue gun to attach the gold braid around the opening of the frame, cutting a mitre and butting at each corner.

Lightly draw a pattern onto the front section of the frame. Refer to the photograph for ideas. Trace over the pencil lines with the hot glue gun, applying the lines in varied thicknesses to provide an interesting effect. With the glue gun, apply a thick line around the outer edge of the gold braid which is already attached. Lightly and evenly spray the frame with gold paint. Using the glue gun re-apply the back section of the frame to the front.

Place the gold mesh ribbon over the basket and glue at the back to hold. Position and glue the covered

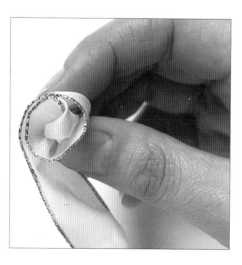

basket at the base of the frame opening. Glue the gold cord around the basket cutout and extend at the top as the handle, begin and end at the top edge of the basket so that the ends of the cord will be fully covered by the flowers.

Make five ribbon roses from each of the green, pink and cream wire-edged ribbons. Cut a 12" (30cm) length, fold one end over at a 45° angle. Roll and push the ribbon at the same time to create a rose shape, secure each rose with florists' wire.

Use the glue gun to glue the flowers in a cascading arrangement at the top of the basket. Cut the pearl yardage into two equal lengths. Roll into a circle and glue to hold. Glue amongst the flowers. Tie a bow from the remaining green ribbon and attach at the centre of the basket. Glue the brass locket charm over the ribbon.

Tie a small bow with trailing tails from the gold ribbon. Glue it to the top right corner of the frame and, using small dabs of glue, attach the trailing tails at a few different points to hold them in place.

To complete the scene, lightly spray gold paint over the entire basket and its contents.

MAKING RIBBON ROSES
The corner of the ribbon is folded down to form the centre of the rose, then the remaining ribbon is curled around it until you have a rose of the desired size.

CROCHETED TOWEL EDGINGS

Mothers and Grandmothers the world over will be touched by the trouble you have taken to create these beautifully edged towels just for their enjoyment. Each birthday or Mothers' Day can be a reason to add yet another matching piece to the set which you can gradually build up and give over the years.

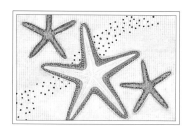

MATERIALS NEEDED

- *Coats Pellicano 2 x 2oz (50g) balls (white)*
- *no. 14 (2.00mm) crochet hook*
- *bath towel, hand towel, face cloth*
- *needle & matching thread*

It is important to use the yarn specified for these edgings as other yarns may give unsatisfactory results.

The quantities given are approximate as they vary between crochet workers.

If you wish to decorate a larger towel you will need extra yarn.

TOWEL EDGINGS
Towel edgings can be crocheted in a darker or lighter shade than the towel or in a contrasting color which will complement or offset the towel's color.

ABBREVIATIONS

ch = chain, sl st = slip stitch, dc = double crochet, tr = treble, sp = space, 'group' = (3 tr, 2 ch, 3 tr) in same sp, beg = beginning.

EDGING MEASUREMENTS

Bath Towel	Hand Towel	Face Cloth
Width		
3" (8cm)	2½" (6cm)	1½" (4cm)
Length		
2' (60cm)	16" (40cm)	13" (33cm)

Make 24 (17-10) ch loosely.

1st row: (Miss 5 ch, 3 tr in next ch, 2 ch, 3 tr in next ch, 1 ch) 3 (2-1) time/s, miss 2 ch, 1 tr in last ch.

2nd row: (1 dc, 1 ch) in first tr, (1 ch, 'group' in centre sp of group) 3 (2-1) time/s, turn.

3rd row: 6 ch, ('group' in centre sp of group, 1 ch) 3 (2-1) time/s, 1 tr in 2nd ch of turning ch loop.

4th row: (1 dc, 1 ch) in first tr, (1 ch, 'group' in centre sp of group) 3 (2-1) time/s, (1 ch, 1 tr) 7 times in 6 ch loop, sl st in each of first 3 ch in the 1st row.

5th-7th rows: 2 ch, 1 dc in next 1 ch sp, (5 ch, 1 dc in next 1 ch sp) 6 times, 3 ch, ('group' in centre sp of group, 1 ch) 3 (2-1) time/s, 1 tr in 2nd ch of turning ch loop. Rep 2nd and 3rd rows once each.

8th row: As 4th row, but sl st in each ch of 3 ch loop of 5th row. Rows 5 to 8 incl form patt.

Cont in patt until the work measures about 60 (40-33) cm (or length desired) from beg, ending with an 8th row.

Next row: 2 ch, 1 dc in next 1 ch sp, (5 ch, 1 dc in next 1 ch sp) 6 times, 3 ch, (2 dc in centre sp of group, 5 ch) 2 (1-0) time/s, 2 dc in centre sp of group, 2 ch, 1 tr in 2nd ch of turning ch loop. Fasten off.

Last row: With right side facing, work 1 row dc evenly along straight section of ends and straight edge, taking care not to stretch your work.

FINISHING OFF

Using a matching thread, sew the completed edgings around each of the towels and the face cloth.

PAINTED VEGETABLE KITCHEN TILES

To celebrate the harvest festival, paint simple designs to create these cheerful tiles, perfect for brightening up a kitchen. They would also be well received for a birthday or house warming gift.

MATERIALS NEEDED

- *glass paints:*
  diox purple, carbon black, pine green, moss green, burgundy, yellow light, napthol red light, French blue (or you can use acrylic paints with a glass and tile painting medium)
- *tracing paper & pencil*
- *carbon paper & stylus*
- *6" x 6" (15cm x 15cm) white tiles*
- *brushes: no.10 round, no.4 round, no.1 round, large flat*
- *water-based satin sealer*
- *wooden frames to fit around tiles*
- *milk paints: country blue, warm olive, red earth*
- *patina wax*
- *soft cloth*
- *spatula*
- *craft glue*

You can use the glass paints in the colors specified, or if you prefer you can work with a mixture of acrylic paints and a glass and tile painting medium. Add the glass and tile medium to the acrylic paints according to the manufacturer's instructions and mix until the glass and tile painting medium has completely blended into the paint.

EGGPLANTS

Trace the design for the eggplants (aubergines) from the pattern section and lightly transfer it onto a clean, dry tile using the carbon paper and stylus.

Add a small amount of carbon black to diox purple to darken it slightly. (Mix in the tile painting medium if using acrylic paint.) To paint the eggplant in the background, load the no.10 round brush with the purple mix. Starting at the top, paint the eggplant using four downward strokes, following the curve of the eggplant shape. Ensure that the brush is well loaded with paint before each stroke.

Paint the eggplant which is in the foreground by starting in the middle and painting two downward strokes. Reload the brush and, starting from the top, move the brush down and around the outline of the eggplant finishing on the opposite side.

Using the large end of the stylus, outline the eggplants and scratch in

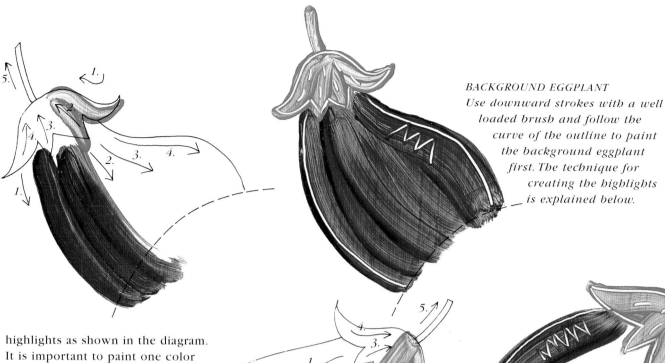

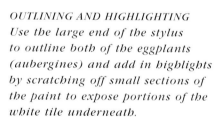

BACKGROUND EGGPLANT
Use downward strokes with a well loaded brush and follow the curve of the outline to paint the background eggplant first. The technique for creating the highlights is explained below.

highlights as shown in the diagram. It is important to paint one color and outline it before continuing on with the next section, if the paint is allowed to dry completely the stylus will 'tear' the paint.

Mix equal parts of pine green and moss green plus any required glass and tile painting medium. Paint the stems and sepals of the eggplants using the no.4 round brush. Allow to dry slightly then outline with the stylus, adding small dashes as shown here.

Paint alternate squares on the tile using burgundy. Use the stylus to scratch random highlights onto some of the burgundy squares.

To paint the background of the design, use the no.10 round brush and only a small amount of yellow light to create a pale shade.

Radishes

Trace the radishes design from the pattern section and lightly transfer it onto a clean, dry tile using the carbon paper and the stylus.

Mix napthol red light with glass and tile painting medium if it is required. Paint the radishes with the no.10 round brush using thick, downward strokes. Using carbon black, add shading around the tops

of the radishes.

Outline and scratch in some highlights using the stylus. Use a mixture of pine green, moss green and yellow light randomly to paint the leaves. Add shading using carbon black. Using the stylus, outline the leaves and draw a stem in the middle of each of the leaves.

Paint alternate squares on the tile using French blue. Scratch in highlights using the stylus.

Paint the background of the design using the no.10 round brush and a small amount of yellow light to create a pale shade.

PAINTING AND OUTLINING
Use pine green, moss green and yellow light randomly to paint the leaves. Draw in the stems and outlines using the stylus.

OUTLINING AND HIGHLIGHTING
Use the large end of the stylus to outline both of the eggplants (aubergines) and add in highlights by scratching off small sections of the paint to expose portions of the white tile underneath.

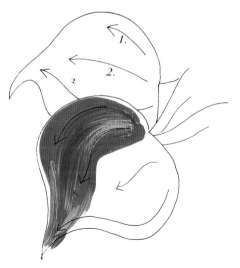

TOMATOES

Trace the tomatoes design from the pattern section and lightly transfer it onto a clean, dry tile using the carbon paper and the stylus.

Paint the tomatoes using the no.10 round brush and napthol red light. Start at the bottom of each tomato, working upwards in thick strokes. Reload the brush after each stroke. Add shading using carbon black. Use the stylus to outline the tomatoes and scratch in highlights.

Use pine green and the no.1 round brush to paint the small leaves and carbon black to add some shading.

Paint alternate squares on the tile using pine green. Highlight some of the squares by scratching with the stylus.

PAINTING THE TOMATOES
Paint the tomatoes using a series of upward strokes. Outline and highlight as shown, using the stylus.

Paint the background of the design using the no.10 round brush and a small amount of yellow light to create a pale shade.

HEAT SETTING

The painted tiles must be heat set. Place the tiles into a cold domestic oven and set to 325°F (165°C). When the temperature is reached, heat cure for 45 minutes.

Leave the tiles in the oven until they have all completely cooled.

When the tiles have cooled, apply one coat of sealer over each of the tiles. Allow to dry before inserting them into the wooden frames.

FRAMES

Milk paints, with their soft looking finish, perfectly complement this style of painting and they do not require any messy pre-mixing. The first coat acts as a primer and the second coat provides solid coverage.

Using milk paint and the large, flat brush, apply one coat of warm olive paint to one of the wooden frames. Allow to dry overnight before applying a second coat. Paint the other two frames using country blue and red earth milk paints.

Using a soft cloth, apply the patina wax to the frame. Allow to dry then buff with a clean area of the cloth. The waxed finish gives a soft, mellow look to the frame. Or, if you prefer, the painted frame can be sealed using a sealer.

Using a spatula and craft glue, apply the glue liberally to the centre of each frame. Place the eggplants (aubergine) into the warm olive frame, the radishes into the country blue frame and the tomatoes into the red earth frame. Press them down and hold in place with a weight until the glue has set fully.

CRACKLED CHERUB BOX

This elegant box is the perfect container to house treasures and would make a lovely gift for some special occasion, such as a bridal shower, or a coming of age gift for a young lady.

MATERIALS NEEDED

- *semi-circular wooden box*
- *damp cloth*
- *medium grade sandpaper*
- *small bisque cherub*
- *craft glue*
- *2 small white tassels*
- *16" (40cm) of thick white cord*
- *plaster of Paris*
- *mixing bowl & spoon*
- *wood sealer*
- *acrylic paints: French blue, gold, off-white*
- *brushes: medium flat, no. 5 round (or similar)*
- *crackle medium*
- *satin sealer*

Sand the entire box, inside and out, with sandpaper and wipe off dust with a damp cloth. Using the craft glue, attach the cherub to the centre of the box lid, allow to dry.

Following the manufacturer's instructions, mix up plaster of Paris using extra water to create a very liquid mixture. Soak the tassels and cord in the plaster. If it does not seem to be soaking in, the mixture is probably too thick: add more water.

Remove the tassels and cord from the plaster and position onto the box lid, draping around the cherub. Allow to dry overnight.

Mix sealer into the French blue at a ratio of 1:1 and, using the flat brush, basecoat the box, applying two coats to satisfactorily seal the craft wood surfaces. Allow to dry.

Using the no.5 round brush, paint gold over the cord, tassels and cherub. Apply two coats if needed. Allow the pieces to dry.

Following the manufacturer's instructions, apply a coat of crackle over the entire box, including the cherub, tassels and cord, but not to the base of the box. Allow to dry.

Paint over the crackle with off-white, using quick short strokes and never going over an area twice. Apply the paint in varying directions as the cracks will appear along the lines of the brush strokes. If the paint is applied in long straight strokes the cracks will not appear varied and natural. Leave to dry.

Using a damp cloth, carefully rub back parts of the crackle from the cord, cherub and tassels. Do not completely rub it off, as it looks natural to have varying depths of crackled paint over those surfaces.

Using sandpaper, gently rub over some areas to 'distress' the paint back to the blue color. Do this in the areas where wear would be most likely, such as the edges, sides and front. Apply two coats of sealer, allow to dry fully between coats.

PAINTING THE BOX
Paint the off-white over the crackle medium in various directions.

DISTRESSING THE BOX
Rub back some paint in areas where the box would naturally be worn.

EDIBLE GIFTS FRESH FROM THE GARDEN

These delicious taste bud pleasers will be a sure winner with anyone who enjoys homemade gourmet goodies. They are just the thing to give at Christmas, for a house warming, or to that person who seems to have everything but still deserves a handmade gift.

FLAVORED OIL

Heat the oil in a double saucepan until it is warm, not hot, and add the mixed chopped herbs, garlic and chilies. Remove from the heat and cover. Allow the oil to stand for five days. Strain and pour the oil into a sterilised bottle.

Replace the garlic and chili and add sprigs of fresh herbs. Cork the bottle. Apply a label with instructions to store the flavored oil in a cool place until needed for use.

LEMON & LIME BUTTER

Makes 3 x 8 fl oz (250ml) jars
Melt the butter and sugar in a double saucepan over a moderate heat. Add the juices, rinds, and eggs, while stirring continuously. Continue to stir the mixture until it thickens enough to coat the back of a spoon, this can take up to 35 minutes. Pour into hot sterilised jars and seal and label when the jars are cool.

ROSE VINEGAR

Place the rose petals in the bottom of a 2pt (1l) jar and pour the vinegar over. Let the jar stand in the sun for two weeks. Strain the vinegar through filter paper. Add in more fresh rose petals and seal.

The same method can be used to make other vinegars and they will need to be allowed to stand for at least five days. As with the rose vinegar, fresh sprigs of the herb used for flavoring can be added for display when re-bottling.

SAVORY MARMALADE

Remove the seeds from the washed red bell peppers (capsicums) and chop them in a food processor. Be careful not to puree them! Stir in the salt and allow to stand for two hours.

Drain the excess liquid from the bell peppers and add the cider vinegar and sugar. Place the mix in a saucepan and bring to the boil before simmering for 1½ hours. Bottle in hot sterilised jars and seal and label the jars when cool.

PRESENTATION

If you re-use attractive jars to hold these scrumptious edibles the finished products will look as good as they taste. You can also add ornamental finishing touches such as bows, seasonal stickers and fabric circles to cover the lids.

When giving these delicious goodies as gifts, apply a decorative label to each finished jar. The labels could be cut into special shapes then colored in and enhanced to suit.

Make sure you include the date on which each item was made, e.g. January 1998, and any special instructions or suggestions for storage or use.

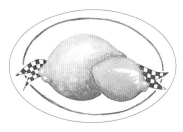

MATERIALS NEEDED

FLAVORED OIL
- *2 cups olive oil*
- *2-3 tbsp mixed fresh herbs, chopped*
- *2-3 cloves garlic*
- *2-3 fresh whole chilies*
- *fresh sprigs of rosemary, tarragon, or herbs of your choice*

LEMON & LIME BUTTER
- *6oz (180g) butter*
- *2 cups sugar*
- *½ cup lemon juice*
- *½ cup lime juice*
- *1 tsp grated lemon & lime rind*
- *4 eggs, beaten & strained*

ROSE VINEGAR
- *2pts (1l) distilled white vinegar*
- *1 cup fresh rose petals*
- *filter paper*

SAVORY MARMALADE
- *3lbs (1.25kg) red bell peppers (capsicums)*
- *1 tsp salt*
- *1 cup cider vinegar*
- *2 cups sugar*

DECORATED BOTTLES

Give a double gift by filling these decorated bottles with some of your homemade edibles. The bottles can also be given just as attractive ornaments and would be most appreciated as a present to celebrate a birthday, wedding, new neighbor welcome, or for Christmas.

MATERIALS NEEDED

PAINTED BOTTLES
- *recycled glass bottles*
- *glass paints: blue, violet, green*
- *brush*
- *relief paints: deep gold, light gold, black*

CHARM DECKED BOTTLES
- *assorted colored glass bottles*
- *brass charms*
- *thin gold cord*
- *hot glue gun*
- *glitter glue sticks*

PAINTED BOTTLES

The bottles used here are an assortment of recycled oil, sauce and vinegar bottles. Clean them thoroughly by washing in warm soapy water. Rinse and dry.

Use a brush to apply the paint to the outside of the bottles. Allow them to dry and apply more coats as needed. Some colors may need to be applied up to four times each before you will achieve a satisfactory depth of color.

When the basecoat of color has dried, apply your selection of designs to the bottles using a combination of the deep gold and the light gold with the black relief paint as outline.

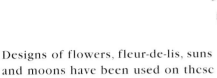

Designs of flowers, fleur-de-lis, suns and moons have been used on these bottles, but of course any designs can be applied.

CHARM DECKED BOTTLES

Ensure the outside surfaces of the bottles are clean and dry by washing them with warm soapy water and allowing them to dry thoroughly.

Use the glue gun to apply the brass charms where desired on the sides of the bottles and some on the tops. The gold glitter glue has a rough texture which creates a strong bond with the smooth surface of glass. Do not worry if the glue seeps through the filigree design of some of the charms as it is gold glitter and will look attractive.

Once the charms have been attached, the finishing touches can be applied. Thread small charms onto thin gold cord and tie around the necks of the bottles. Gold glitter glue can be applied directly to the

bottles, especially around their necks, to decorate them further.

Small plaques can also be hung from the neck and charms glued on.

The completed bottles should not be immersed in water, but can be wiped over with a damp cloth.

SIMPLE AND DELIGHTFUL DESIGNS
Many designs are quick and simple to do yet will give your finished work a delightful, naive appearance. Don't worry about drawing all the designs identically, slight variations will add to the handmade charm of the piece.

USING RELIEF PAINTS
Relief paints come with a nozzle which allows you to paint the design directly onto the surface without the need for brushes or nibs. They give a wonderful raised and textured finish and are ideal for using on curved surfaces.

$\mathcal{B}$ATHTIME $\mathcal{F}$UN

What better way to welcome new babies into the world than by giving them their own handmade matching towel and face cloth set. These delightful cross stitched designs use bright primary colors and would also be a welcome gift for any Christening or baby naming celebration.

MATERIALS NEEDED

HOME LINEN SET
- *blue bath towel and face cloth*
- *14 count aida band: 2" x 30", 1" x 16" (5cm x 75cm, 2.5cm x 40cm)*
- *Anchor stranded cotton: (1 skein each) 132, 335, 297, 227, 944, 399, 403*

TRAIN LINEN SET
- *white bath towel and face cloth*
- *14 count aida band: 2" x 30", 1" x 16" (5cm x 75cm, 2.5cm x 40cm)*
- *Anchor stranded cotton: (1 skein each) 132, 335, 297, 227, 944, 403, 881, 140*

The lengths given above are sufficient to make one strip along the bottom of a towel and face cloth.

The cross stitch design is worked throughout with three strands of embroidery yarn. Each square on the design chart represents one cross stitch and each symbol represents the color of thread to use.

Do not begin your work with a knot, instead, select a thread, hold the loose end behind the fabric and secure it in place with the first few cross stitches. To end off a thread, run the needle through the back of several stitches to secure it.

All cross stitches should be worked in the same direction. Try to keep your tension even and do not pull the thread too tightly. This fabric can be worked with or without an embroidery hoop.

Should the work become soiled, wash it in mild soap. Rinse well and dry flat. Do not wring. Press from the back with a warm iron.

When the cross stitch is complete, place the strip on the towel or face cloth, allowing about 1/2" (1cm) extra on the edge to turn under for a finished edge. Sew into place by machine or with a fine back stitch along the edge.

CROSS STITCH
You can work cross stitch either from right to left or from left to right, however, it is important that the upper part of all crosses be done in the same direction. Each stitch is formed around the four corners of a square. To begin you stitch all the half stitches going in one direction to the end of the row. Then complete the upper half of the cross as shown.

$\mathcal{H}$OME LINEN SET

To make the towel trim, use 2" (5cm) wide aida band and commence work from the edge leaving about 1 1/2" (4cm) at the start.

Work from the graph which is located in the pattern section, and repeat the home design to the required length to fit the size of your towel.

Work the 1" (2.5cm) wide aida band for the face cloth in the same way as described for the towel.

$\mathcal{T}$RAIN LINEN SET

To make the towel trim, use 2" (5cm) wide aida band and commence work from the edge leaving about 1 1/2" (4cm) at the start.

Work from the graph which is located in the pattern section, and repeat the train design to the required length to fit your towel.

The links joining the train's carriages are worked using back stitch in three strands of black.

Work the 1" (2.5cm) wide aida band for the face cloth in the same way as described for the towel.

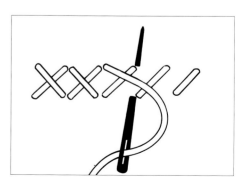

KNITTED LACE CARNATIONS

Bringing a gift of flowers for the hostess is a longstanding tradition in many countries around the world. These bright red carnations make a pretty gift that will last long after your visit is over and, what's more, they don't ever need watering!

TO MAKE
Cast on 18 stitches.
1st-5th rows: Knit 5 rows.
6th row: Knit 1, increase, repeat (27 stitches).
7th row: Knit in lace.
8th-10th rows: Knit 3 rows.
11th row: Knit in lace.
12th-13th rows: Knit 2 rows.
14th row: Knit 1, decrease, repeat (18 stitches).
15th row: Knit in lace.
16th row: Knit 2 together across (9 stitches).
17th row: Knit 3, Knit 1 through 3 holes (eyelets) of lace, Knit 3, Knit 1 through 3 holes, Knit 1.
18th row: Knit 2 together across, Knit 1 (5 stitches).

Draw up stitches and sew the seam. Stuff lightly and gather onto the stem. If the silk stems have been purchased as actual silk flowers, remove the silk flowers. Glue each knitted carnation onto a stem to secure it in place.

Silk carnation stems are available at craft stores. Alternatively you can purchase inexpensive silk carnations and remove the heads so that the stems can be re-used for your knitted lace flowers.

MATERIALS NEEDED
- 8 ply red yarn
- no.8 (3.75mm) needles
- 1¼ yds (1m) of red eyelet lace
- polyester filling
- needle & matching thread
- carnation stems

$\mathcal{M}$OSAIC $\mathcal{M}$IRROR
To celebrate some marvellous success, such as a graduation, a promotion, or an impending marriage, you can give this gift to constantly remind the receiver just who it is that you admire.

MATERIALS NEEDED

- *4" x 8" (10cm x 20cm) ceramic tiles*
- *16¹/₂" x 16¹/₂" (42cm x 42cm) wooden board*
- *8" x 8" (20cm x 20cm) mirror*
- *glass and tile paints: purple, yellow, pine green, bright purple*
- *brushes: flat, round*
- *hammer*
- *cloth*
- *sheet of clear adhesive paper*
- *tile adhesive*
- *white tile grout*
- *spatula*
- *stylus*

PAINTING THE TILES
We have painted the designs onto each tile separately then lined each one up with the next tile to ensure the designs fit together and the outlines match up with the adjoining tiles.

Tiles come in a variety of sizes and shapes. If you cannot locate the size used here, use whatever size is available to you, matching the size of the board to fit. When selecting the size of the board ensure that it is slightly larger than the area covered by the tiles. This is to allow for the spacing between the tiles when they are broken to form the mosaic.

You can either paint the tiles individually—ensure you line up the design where it overlaps the next tile—or, to simplify the method, place all the tiles together (as if positioned around the board) and paint the whole design over all the tiles. Refer to the photograph to see the design. This is a simple design to draw freehand but you may like to practise drawing it first on a piece of paper.

Using purple and the flat brush, paint the inner and outer rims of the design and allow to dry. Using yellow, paint the middle strip of the design, leaving a ¹/₄" (6mm) gap between both sides of the purple borders.

Using the large end of the stylus, engrave the swirls around the purple.

Ensure the yellow paint is completely dry before painting the tulip design. Paint the tulips randomly around all the tiles using bright purple. Leave enough space between each tulip to add the leaf and stem. Use pine green plus yellow to paint the stems. Paint one leaf on each stem, alternating the sides on which you paint them. Allow to dry then use the stylus to engrave the detail on each of the leaves.

When the tiles have dried, they must be baked in an oven to achieve a more durable glaze. Place the tiles in a cool oven and set it to 325°F (165°C). Bake the tiles in the oven for 40 minutes, allowing them to cool before removing from the oven.

Place the tiles on a soft surface, such as a wad of newspaper, as a hard surface may cause the tiles to break too much. Place a cloth over the tiles to avoid any tile splinters from flying up and to prevent the hammer from damaging the painted surface. Use a hammer to crack the tiles, ensuring there is a mixture of both large and small pieces. If any areas of the design chip, they can be retouched with paint but if a more distressed look is desired, as for this mirror, leave them chipped.

Position the tile pieces on the board to form the mosaic, spacing them to fit the size of the board. It is important to lay out the whole design before gluing it in place.

Remove the adhesive paper from its backing. Press the adhesive side of the paper onto its backing sheet to remove the excess stickiness. Place the adhesive paper over the broken mosaic pieces and smooth the paper down with your hand, ensuring that all the mosaic pieces are firmly

attached. Lift the paper and mosaic pieces from the surface of the board and set aside.

Using a spatula, apply the tile adhesive to the entire board. Pick up the paper and tiles and position them over the board, lining up the outer edges. Place the tiles down onto the glued board, smoothing over the paper to encourage the tiles to stick to the glue. Carefully, peel back the paper and remove.

Press down on each piece of the mosaic ensuring it is firmly attached. Allow to dry.

Before applying grout to the spaces in between the tiles, you may like to apply a coat of sealer to protect your design. For this project, the tiles were left unsealed as a softer, distressed look was what we were aiming for here.

Mix the grout with water to achieve a toothpaste consistency.

Using a spatula, cover the mosaic design completely with grout. Use the edge of the spatula to remove the excess grout from the top of the tiles. Wipe the surface of all the tiles with a damp cloth, removing the remaining excess grout.

Glue the mirror into position on the board. Any gap around the mirror can be filled in with grout. Allow the grout to dry. Paint the outside edge of the frame in purple.

63

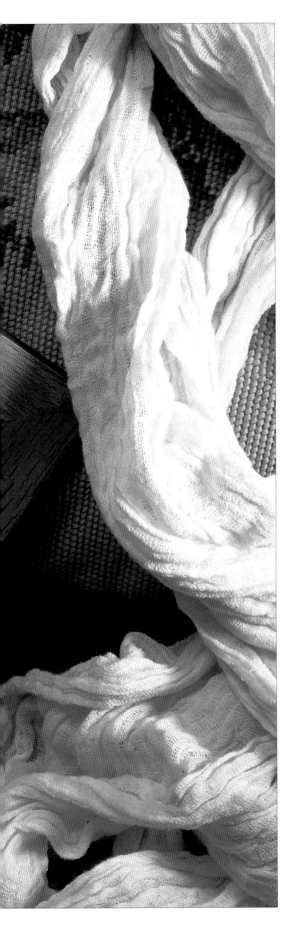

CRACKLED PHOTO FRAME

When a special occasion deserves marking, you can make this rustic timber frame and give it as a gift with a suitable photograph already in place.

Paint the frame with leaf green basecoat. Allow the paint to dry after the first coat and then sand lightly before applying the second coat of paint. Leave to dry.

The crackle medium is applied to two sides at a time to achieve the look of joined timber. Mask off two sides and apply crackle medium to the other two. Use the sponge brush to apply long definite strokes of crackle medium. The thicker this is applied, the larger the cracks will be, and the thinner it is applied, the smaller the cracks will be.

Once the crackle is dry to touch, usually after about 20 minutes, apply the straw basecoat, using long definite strokes. Allow to dry and apply a coat of sealer. Leave to dry completely.

Remove the masking tape and mask off the sides that have already been completed.

Apply the crackle medium and straw basecoat in the same manner as it was applied to the first two sides. Apply sealer as before also. Allow to dry completely.

Using the soft cloth, rub the antiquing medium over the frame. Using the same section of the cloth, rub the burnt umber over the frame. Using a clean section of the cloth, rub back the burnt umber. Leave for 24 hours then apply a coat of sealer to seal the finished piece. Allow the frame to dry thoroughly before fitting in a photo of your choice.

MATERIALS NEEDED

- *timber photo frame*
- *acrylic basecoat paints: leaf green, straw*
- *crackle medium*
- *masking tape*
- *burnt umber oil paint*
- *oil-based antiquing medium*
- *sealer*
- *2 sponge brushes*
- *soft cloth*

GILDED CANDLE BOX

Candles add a glorious romantic glow to any special occasion. A beautifully ornamented and gilded box, such as this one, makes the ideal place to safely store candles for use. This gift is perfect for any romantically inclined person or event.

MATERIALS NEEDED

- *wooden candle box*
- *fine grade sandpaper*
- *tack cloth*
- *craft glue*
- *harp crest molding*
- *sealer or gesso*
- *brushes: basecoating, soft-bristled*
- *acrylic paints: red earth, pale gold, raw umber*
- *water-based size*
- *sea sponge*
- *gold Dutch metal leaf*
- *satin or gloss sealer*
- *a selection of candles (optional)*

Lightly sand the wooden candle box and wipe away the dust using the tack cloth. Using the craft glue, attach the harp crest molding to the center of the lid of the candle box. Press down on the molding so that it will adhere firmly to the box.

Apply one coat of sealer or gesso to all inside and outside surfaces of the box, including the molding. Allow to dry completely.

Lightly sand all surfaces of the box, wiping away the dust.

Basecoat the inside and outside of the top and base of the box with the red earth acrylic paint, applying a second coat if necessary.

When the basecoat is dry, apply one coat of pale gold. This coat may be applied rather roughly; in fact it adds to the finished appeal if the brush strokes are visible. Allow to dry.

Apply small random strokes of size over the outer surfaces of the lid and base of the box using the brush or sea sponge. When the size is tacky, use the tip of a soft-bristled brush to pick up skewings, or small pieces of left over gold leaf, and apply them to the sized areas. Skewings saved from gilding projects should be stored in an air-tight container for use in other projects, such as this one. Tamp the skewings onto the surface using the brush then wipe away any excess.

Using a clean sponge, lightly dab raw umber over the painted surfaces and allow to dry.

To complete the candle box, apply three coats of satin or gloss sealer to the lid and the base, sanding lightly between coats.

Fill the completed box with a selection of beautiful candles to give as a gift. You can select colors that suit the receiver's décor or else just choose a variety of colors to suit many different occasions and moods.

GILDING THE BOX
Apply the skewings to the sized areas and tamp down using the brush.

FINISHING THE BOX
Lightly dab the raw umber paint onto the candle box using the sea sponge.

GIFT WRAPPING IDEAS

WRAPPING PAPERS

CREATING YOUR OWN PATTERNS

There is no reason why your choice
of wrapping papers should be limited
to what you can find in the shops.
It is more economical and unique
to create your own wrapping papers
out of plain papers decorated with
one of these simple craft techniques.

Some of the techniques which
can be used are stamping, stenciling,
painting, embossing, marker pen
drawing and gilding.

This page shows you some of
the papers we created using these
techniques, together with some
elegant and simple designs.

STAMPED FLEUR-DE-LIS
Stamping easily creates a repeated
pattern all over the paper.

STENCILED FLOURISH & PAINTED SHELLS
A stencil and brush give this classic
design, a feature on its own. Hand paint
a variety of designs around a single theme.

GOLD MARKER STARS & GILDED CHERRIES
Quickly and easily, a gold pen lets you
create a stunning yet simple pattern.
For a special touch, you can gild some
of the design elements on the paper.

70

PRE-LOVED PAPERS

Many different types of paper which originally had another purpose can be put to great use as very attractive and versatile wrapping papers.

Here we have re-used sheets of newspaper, sheet music, color pages from a magazine, and an old map, as wrapping papers with a twist. Re-use a style of paper which suits the gift or the recipient.

Drawings and other artistic creations by younger members of the household make excellent gift wrap for presents to be given to doting grandparents and friends.

TEAR AND GLUE

This simple flower design is made by gluing torn scraps of paper on to the wrapped present. Position the flowers to best suit the package.

LAYERED PAPERS

Fine tissue paper can be used in layers with leaves, flower petals. string, or other interesting items, glued in between the sheets.

WRAPPED AND STITCHED

Use some attractive fabric scraps to wrap the present and then seal it by stitching the parcel closed with a decorative stitch and colorful yarn.

FABRIC WRAPPINGS

Fabrics can be used to wrap up the present or they can form a part of the present you are giving, for example you can make up a fabric bag in which to give a gift but which can then be used by the receiver as a handy bag for storage, travel, or carrying items to and fro.

FABRIC WRAPPED BUNDLES

Gingham and gauze are versatile fabrics which are perfect for bundling up unusually shaped parcels. Brightly colored ribbon or other trims can be used to keep the bundles closed.

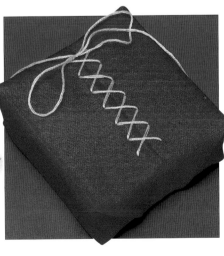

WRAPPING PAPERS INSPIRATION

Here is a range of fabulous wrapping paper ideas to inspire you. The colors and designs shown can easily be adapted to suit personal tastes. Let your designing imagination run wild!

This raised pattern is embossed on the reverse side of the paper.

Glue creates a raised and shiny pattern on tissue paper.

A cherub stamp using white ink or paint will give a striking effect.

Découpage decorations make a wrapping paper with flair.

This traditional Japanese technique uses glued-on torn paper designs.

Color markers let you draw quick and easy patterns across the page.

Layered tissue papers give a subtle and exquisite coloring effect.

Cork cuttings allow you to create a repeat print all over the paper.

Scrunch a sheet of paper, dip it into gold paint and press it on the page.

A glued-on fabric patch is finished off with hand drawn stitches.

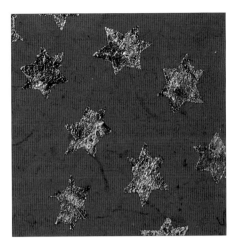

This spray of sparkling stars has been gilded onto the page.

The page glows with a glorious stamp of the sun impressed in gold.

Cut a shaped window in one sheet of paper, glue it to a second sheet.

Paint is flicked from an old tooth-brush through a stencil shape.

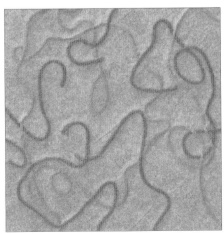

A varied pattern of threads placed between two sheets of tissue paper.

Gild a square on the page around the edges of a cutout shape.

Draw a design on in glue and then apply glitter to the shape.

PAINTING & DECORATING BOXES

Boxes which once held shoes, groceries, or other everyday items can be given a new lease of life as gift boxes if they are covered, or painted and decorated.

When packing fragile gifts in spacious boxes, use some type of filling material to keep them safely in place, such as scrunched tissue paper, cotton wool, pot pourri, shreds of paper, or even popcorn!

ORIGAMI BOX

Refer to the diagram shown (right) and draw a grid of 4 x 4 squares. Draw the diagonal cuts and folds. Fold in number order, fold inward on blue, outward on green and make cuts on purple lines.

Open out. Fold line 11 so that A meets B and C points to the centre of the base. Fold over flap D along the crease 14 line. Repeat with flap E and raise this side of the box to form one side and 2 half sides at right angles to base. Repeat with the opposite side.

Holding the two folded sides roughly in position, pick up flap F and fold it over the nearest side pushing the inside

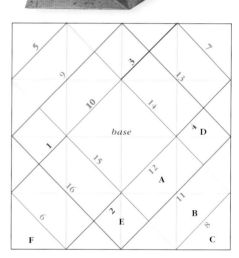

crease down so that the point meets the other two in the centre of the base, and secures the 3 sides. Repeat with the remaining flap to finish the box.

Make a slightly larger box for a lid.

GIFT PACK

Cut the pattern shown here (left) to the required size, score along the lines and fold it to the finished shape.

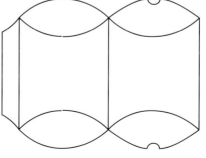

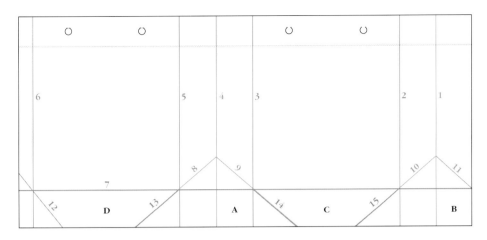

PAPER GIFT BAG

Draw on the creases and fold the bag, in numerical order, creasing inward on green and outward on blue lines. Open the paper out.

Glue the sides of the bag (or use double-sided tape).

Invert the bag and push down areas A and B to begin to create the base of the bag.

Fold down C, then D, securing with double-sided tape. Cut out a base insert (from strong cardboard) to fit and place it inside the base of the bag to provide extra strength.

FABRIC BAG

This bag is just a rectangle of fabric cut to the desired height and twice the desired width.

With right sides of the fabric facing each other, sew a seam across the folded base and up one side. Hem the edges at the neck of the bag.

Turn the bag right side out and attach a cord or ribbon at the neck of the bag to keep it closed.

ENVELOPES

Make your own envelopes in colors, shapes, and sizes to suit your cards or to enclose some of the smaller gifts shown throughout the book.

Select a sheet of paper or thin card and follow the diagrams shown here to create envelopes folded using the diagonal or the square pattern. You may need to score the creases if you use card.

Use paper glue or double-sided tape to hold the folds in position.

Each completed envelope can be decorated with patterns which match the wrapping or the gift in theme, design or color.

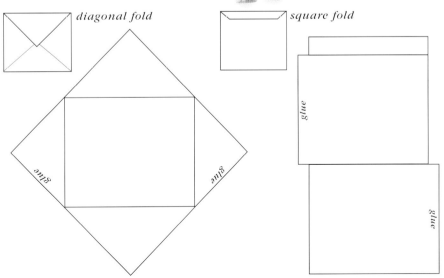

diagonal fold

square fold

TIES & DECORATIONS

RIBBONS & TIES

As well as conventional gift ribbon there are a variety of wonderful tying materials available to suit your gift.

Choose from wire-edged ribbons, satin ribbons, bows and rosettes, embroidery threads, jute, raffia, cord, strips of fabric, strings of beads, chain, and many more possibilities.

Ribbons and other ties can be twisted to unusual effect, tied in interesting ways, used in colorful combinations, and folded in many versatile and attractive shapes and patterns; here are some ideas.

ATTACHING TAGS

Before you attach the gift tag, give some thought to the overall look of your parcel. Sometimes a ring of sticky tape concealed behind the tag gives the best effect, otherwise you may choose to use decorative tape on top, or punch a hole in the tag and attach it to the gift using a matching thread, string or ribbon.

Once the tag is firmly attached to the parcel, you can decorate it in an appropriate way using twirls of ribbon in shades of the same color or in contrasting colors. A sprig of herbs, leaves or blossoms can be tied to the tag for scent and looks.

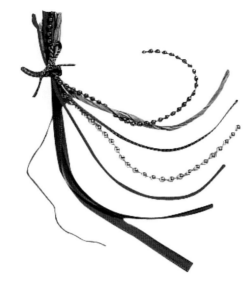

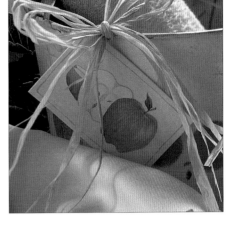

SEASONAL DECORATIONS

Small charms, ornaments, or cutouts can be attached to the gift to highlight the occasion of its giving.

For Christmas: candles, stars, stockings, angels, santas, wreaths, pine cones, and trees express the mood of the season. For Easter: use rabbits and eggs; for new baby gifts: choose from bears, dolls, hearts, and balloons; for romantic occasions, such as Valentine's day, weddings, engagements and anniversaries: some suitable designs are hearts, flowers, rings, bells, horse shoes, doves, and tiered cakes.

DECORATIONS TO GIVE

Some items can play a double role: they can decorate the present and can also be a part of the gift in their own right.

Select fresh, silk, or dried flowers; small toys, balloons, or other tokens which will enhance the presentation of your gift and will also bring even more joy to the lucky receiver.

$\mathcal{T}$IES & DECORATIONS INSPIRATION

An astonishing array of items can be very useful in decorating your gift ready for giving. The ideas shown here will get you started on the path of imaginative and appealing finishes.

Ribbons, roses and pearls provide a classic romantic look.

A more natural look is achieved with green gauze and molded fruits.

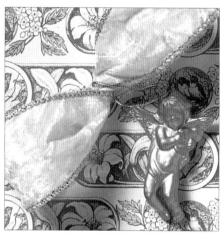

Velvet ribbon and a cherub charm will convey a soft, tender mood.

Natural items like terracotta, string and wheat suggest the country.

Grapes and fleur-de-lis ribbon speak of elegance and enjoyment.

A bright, sunny look is achieved with this colorful decoration.

Felt and velvet combine to give a soft, feminine appearance.

Sun- or oven-dried lemon slices can be tied to the gift with a raffia bow.

Paper ribbon offsets bright dried flowers and a fabric bumble bee.

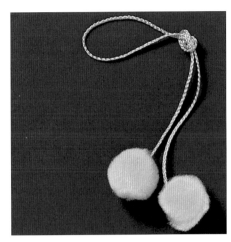

Pom poms make a perky decoration for a parcel and a fun toy for later.

Gingham ribbon and bright molded berries give a cheerful finish.

Shiny tinsels are especially suitable for dressing up Christmas gifts.

A bundle of bright pencils makes an unusual and practical decoration.

Use fresh roses tied with ribbon to give style and scent to your parcel.

Cords and tassels can be used both to tie the parcel and as an ornament.

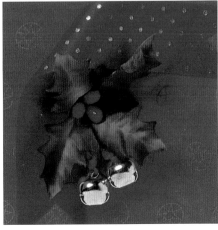

Embellish a corner of your gift with colorful ribbons, bells, and holly.

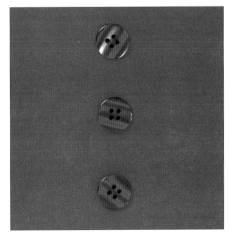

Glue or sew buttons onto a fabric or paper wrap for a fun look.

BLACK TAPESTRY COATHANGER

■	9208 - 1 skein	□	8366 - 1 skein
L	9204 - 1 skein	↑	8364 - 1 skein
N	9174 - 1 skein	•	9800 - 4 skeins
=	9162 - 1 skein	T	8038 - 1 skein
▲	8402 - 1 skein	▼	8040 - 1 skein
X	8420 - 1 skein	●	8042 - 1 skein

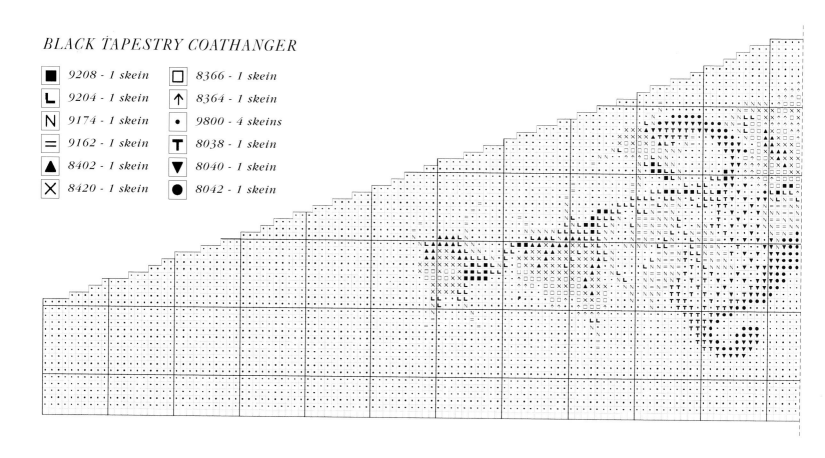

BEIGE TAPESTRY COATHANGER

▼	9208 - 1 skein
X	9204 - 1 skein
—	9174 - 1 skein
U	9162 - 1 skein
T	8402 - 1 skein
N	8420 - 1 skein
=	8366 - 1 skein
+	8364 - 1 skein
•	9402 - 4 skeins
■	8428 - 1 skein

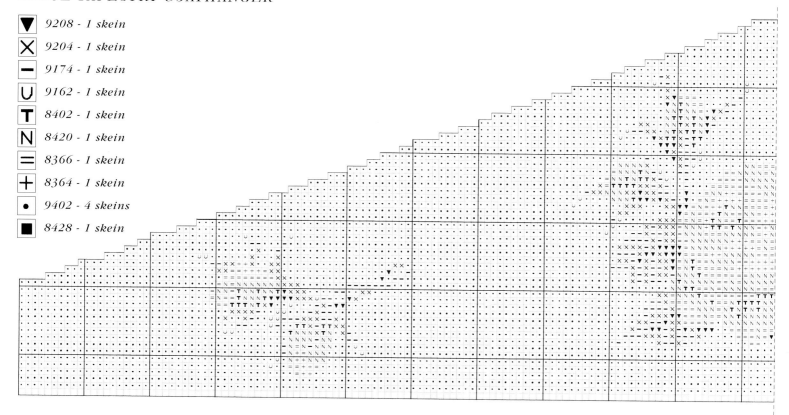

80

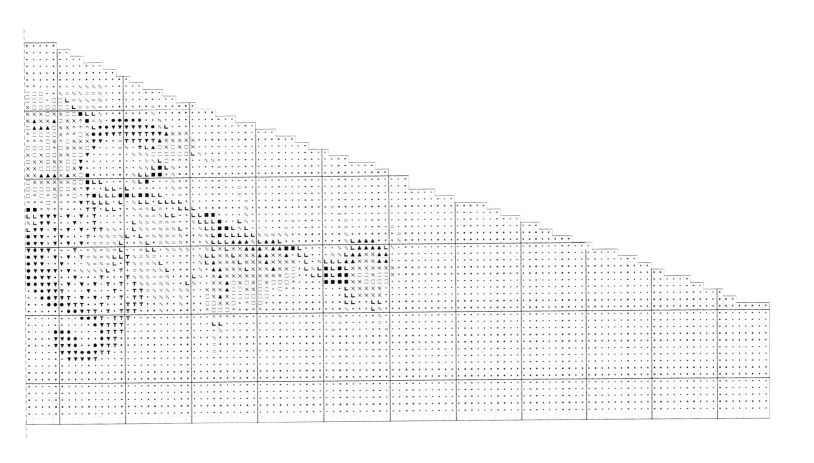

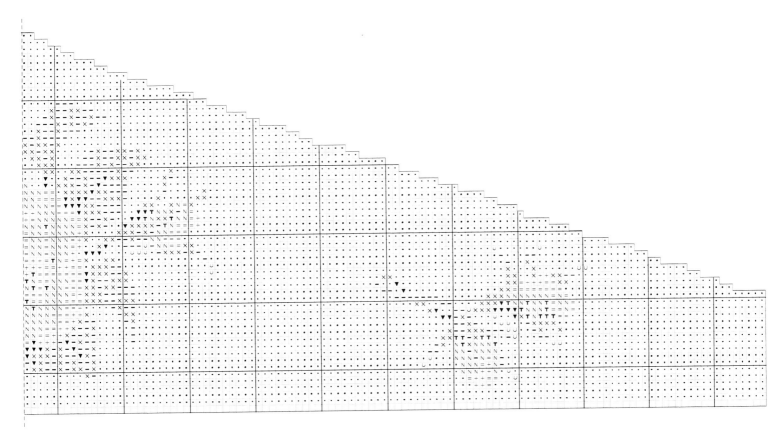

WILBUR PIG

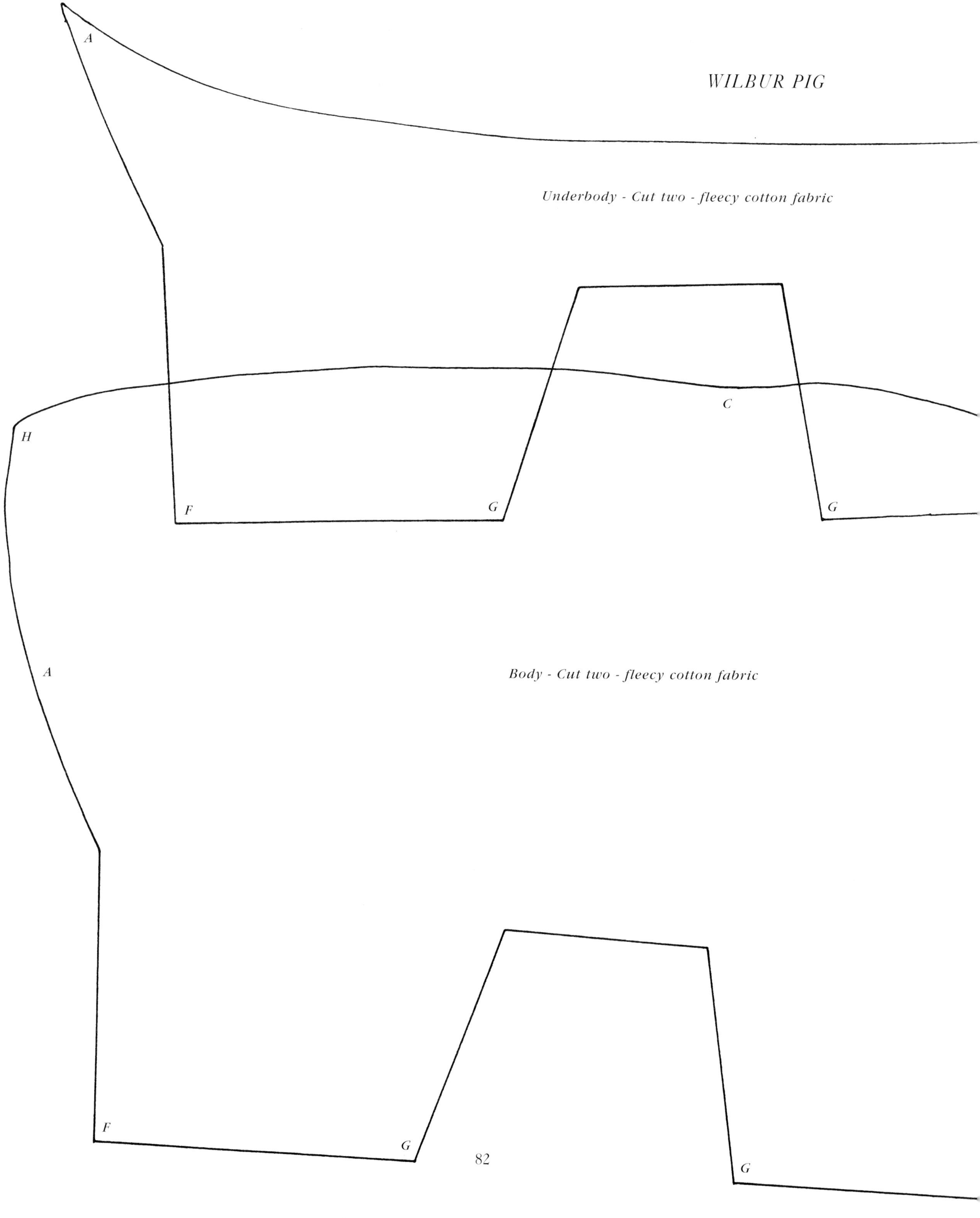

A

Underbody - Cut two - fleecy cotton fabric

C

H

F

G

G

A

Body - Cut two - fleecy cotton fabric

F

G

82

G

G

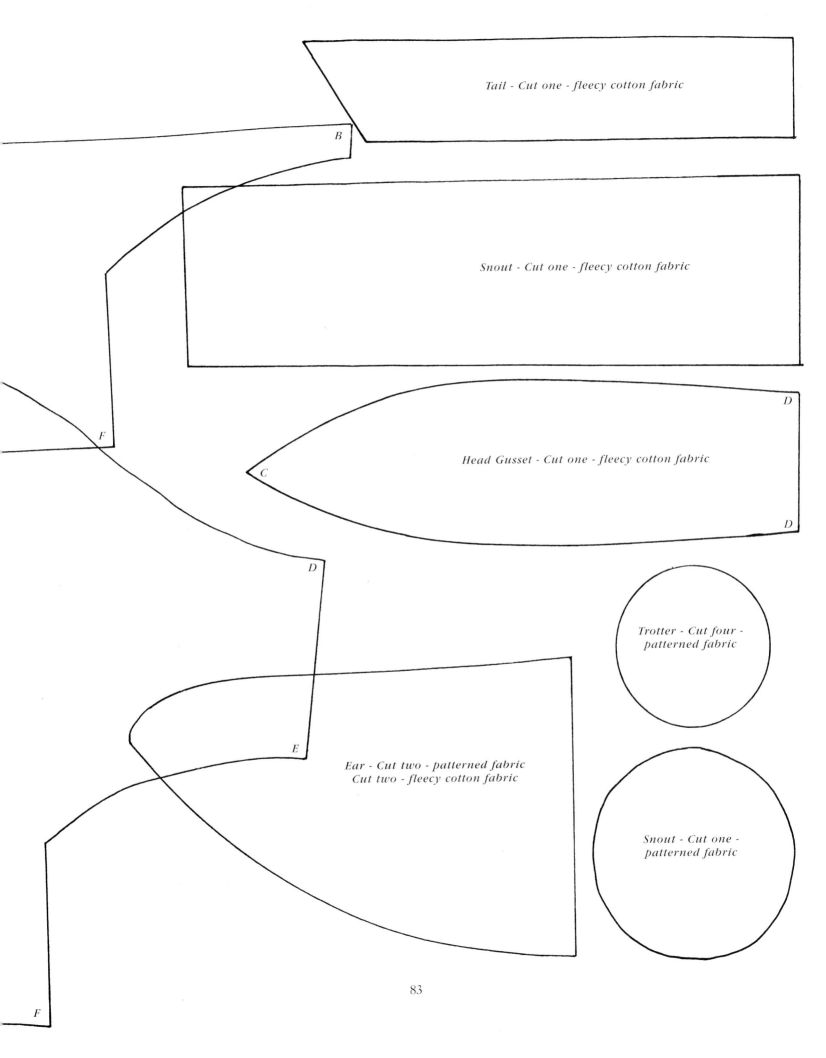

Tail - Cut one - fleecy cotton fabric

Snout - Cut one - fleecy cotton fabric

B

F

D

C

Head Gusset - Cut one - fleecy cotton fabric

D

D

Trotter - Cut four - patterned fabric

E

Ear - Cut two - patterned fabric
Cut two - fleecy cotton fabric

Snout - Cut one - patterned fabric

83

F

Home Linen Set - Towel and Hand Towel``

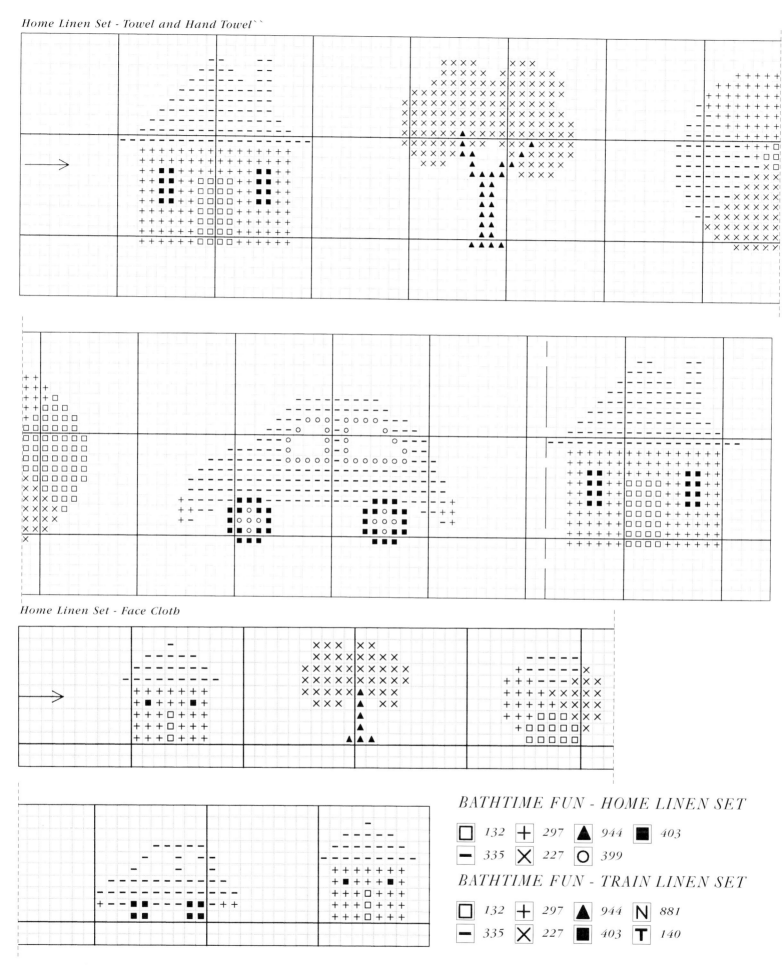

Home Linen Set - Face Cloth

BATHTIME FUN - HOME LINEN SET

□ 132	+ 297	▲ 944	■ 403
− 335	✕ 227	○ 399	

BATHTIME FUN - TRAIN LINEN SET

□ 132	+ 297	▲ 944	N 881
− 335	✕ 227	■ 403	T 140

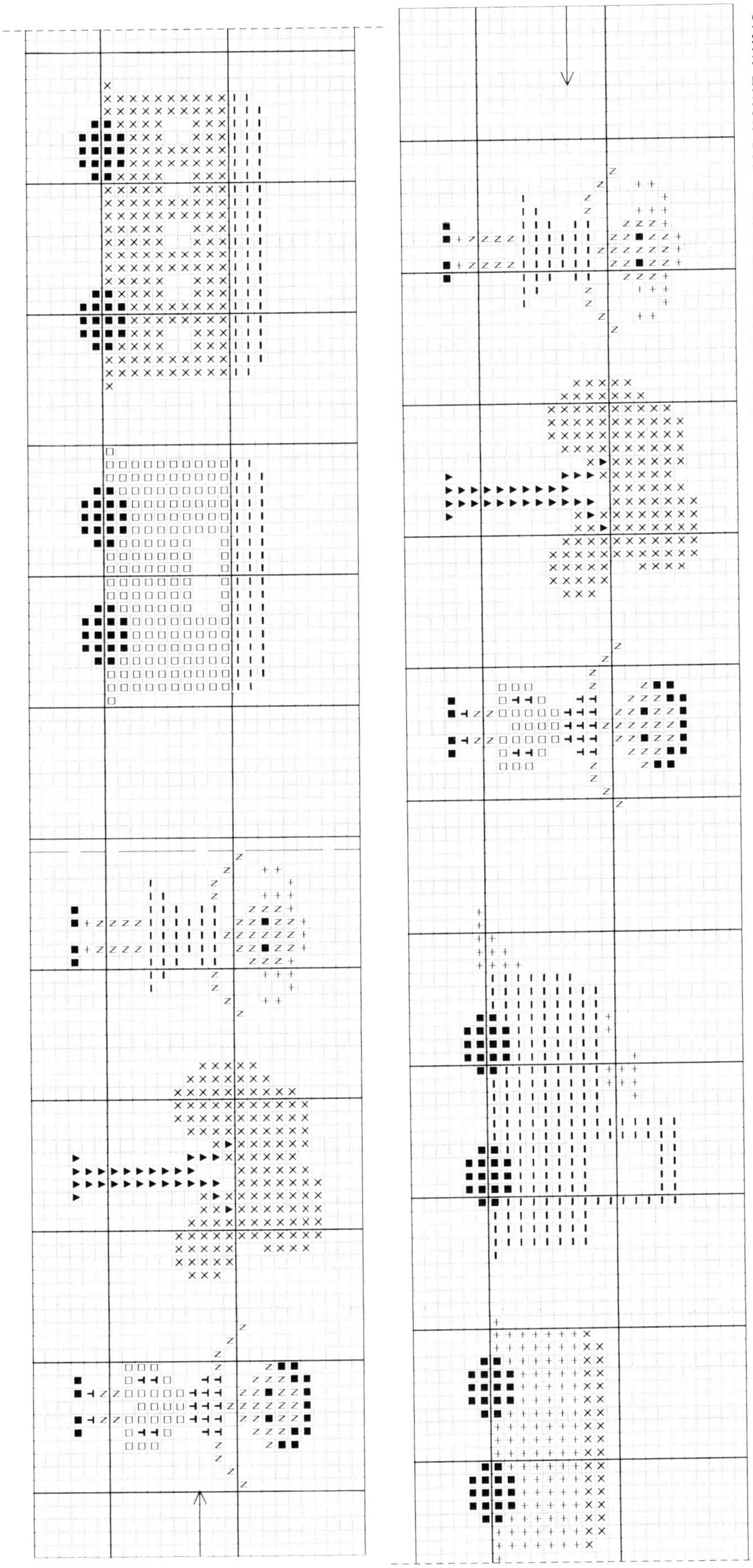

Train Linen Set - Towel and Hand Towel

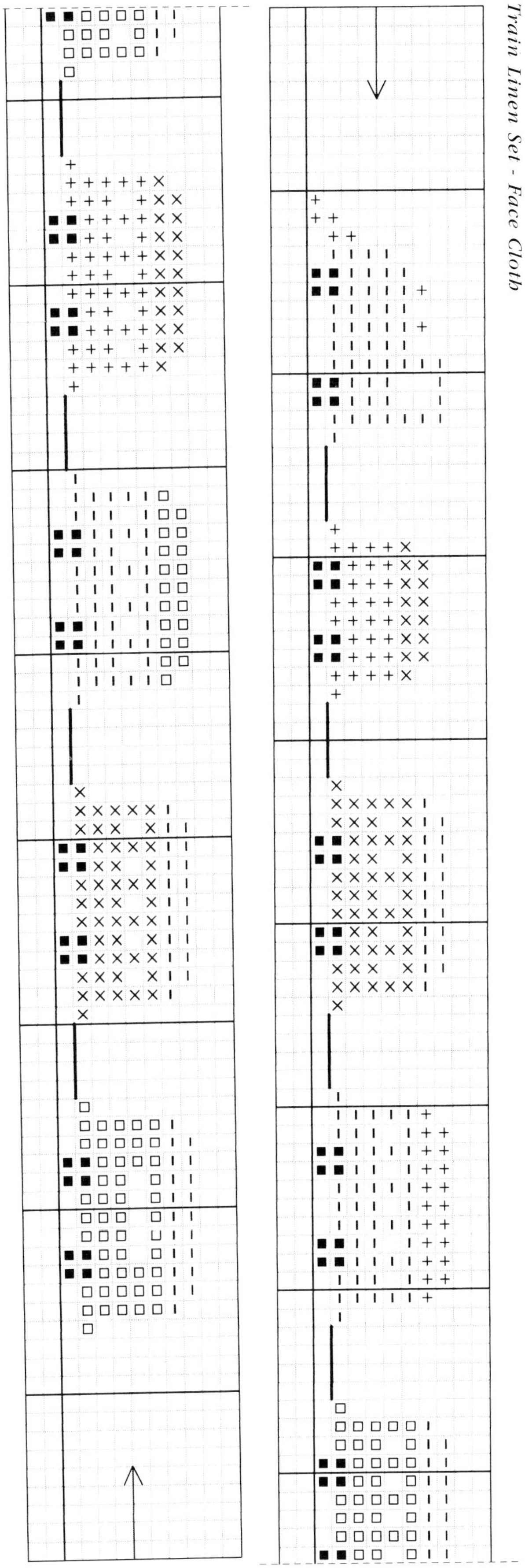

Train Linen Set - Face Cloth

STENCILED BATHROOM SET AT 60%

SCULPTED TERRACOTTA DAISY POTS AT 100%

When you need to enlarge a pattern, use a photocopier and set it to convert the pattern to 100%. For example, a pattern given at 40% should be enlarged by 60% so that it reaches 100%.

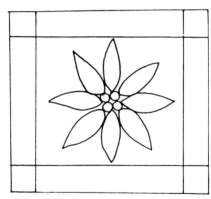

PAINTED GLASSWARE AT 70%

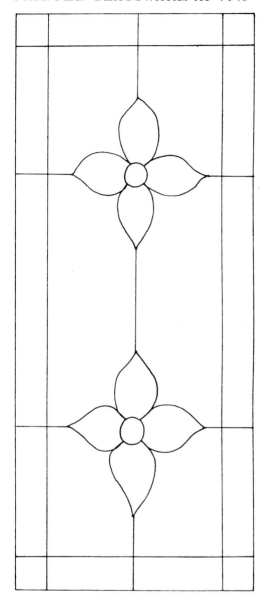

PAINTED VEGETABLE KITCHEN TILES AT 40%

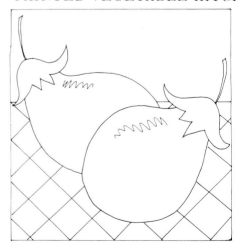

ACKNOWLEDGMENTS

The Publisher gratefully acknowledges the people and organizations (listed here in alphabetical order) who contributed projects shown in this book:

Birch Haberdashery & Craft
153 Bridge Road
Richmond VIC 3121 Australia
Tel: (03) 9429 4944
Fax: (03) 9429 2148
Knitted Lace Carnations
on page 60 by Nance Naisbitt
Wilbur Pig on page 34

Boyle Industries Pty Ltd
Factory 4, 14 Apollo Court
Blackburn VIC 3130 Australia
Tel: (03) 9894 2233
Fax: (03) 9894 2382
Etched Bowl on page 22
by Gina Andrews

Coats Patons Crafts
89-91 Peters Avenue
Mulgrave VIC 3170 Australia
Tel: (03) 9561 2288
Fax: (03) 9561 2298
Bathtime Fun on page 58
Crocheted Towel
Edgings on page 44
Knitted Bears on page 24
Tapestry Coathangers
on page 16

Crafty Things
192 Railway Parade
PO Box 100
Kogarah NSW 2217 Australia
Tel: (02) 9587 4323
Fax: (02) 9587 9403
Bread Dough Forget-me-nots
on page 40 by Liz Bryant

Giftcraft
39-41 Fullarton Road
Kent Town SA 5067 Australia
Tel: (08) 8363 1708
Fax: (08) 8363 2029
Ribbon Rose Basket Victorian
Frame on page 42 and
Decorated Bottles on page 54
both by Marilyn Spanton

Lugarno Craft Cottage
243 Belmore Road
Riverwood NSW 2210 Australia
Tel: (02) 9584 1944
Fax: (02) 9533 1485
Stenciled Bathroom Set on
page 20 by Jo Anne Williamson

Print Blocks Pty Ltd
Stamps & Crafts
441 Waterworks Road
Brisbane (Ashgrove)
QLD 4060 Australia
Tel: (07) 3366 0366
Fax: (07) 3366 0377
Stamp Pad Stenciling on page 36

Rossdale Pty Ltd
PO Box 222 Abbotsford
VIC 3067 Australia
Tel: (03) 9482 3988
Fax: (03) 9482 3874
Sculpted Terracotta
Daisy Pots on page 28

**The Stencil House
Victoria Pty Ltd**
Shop B 103 Lower Mall
Chadstone Shopping Centre
1341 Dandenong Road
Chadstone VIC 3148 Australia
Tel: (03) 9563 0011
Fax: (03) 9563 0022
Gilded Floral Ornaments
on page 12 by Michelle Wright

Tri-Chem Paintcrafts Aust
48 Bellfield Avenue
Rossmore NSW 2171
Australia
Tel: (02) 9606 6963
Fax: (02) 9606 5503
Painted Glassware on page 38

Woodstock Pty Ltd
114 Union Road
Surrey Hills
VIC 3127 Australia
Tel: (03) 9836 4334
Fax: (02) 9836 4334
Personal Stamp Exchange
Stamps shown on pages 70 & 72

GIFT GIVING REGISTER

DATE	PROJECT MADE	GIVEN TO	OCCASION

IMPORTANT DATES TO REMEMBER

DATE	PERSON	OCCASION

Cut carefully just inside the grey outlines. See page 77 for instructions on how to attach tags to gifts.

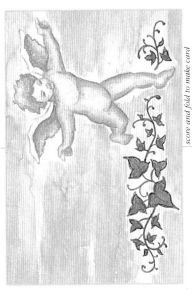

score and fold to make card

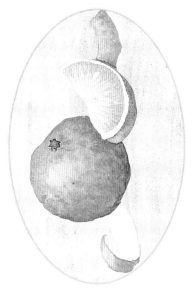

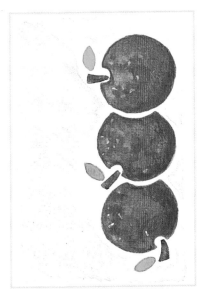

score and fold to make card

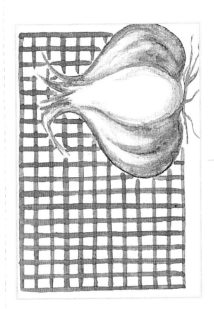

score and fold to make card